To social work students: past, present and future.

Changing Agency Policy

An Incremental Approach

Ann Rae
Saginaw Valley State University

Wanda Nicholas-Wolosuk
University of Michigan–Flint

Boston   New York   San Francisco
Mexico City   Montreal   Toronto   London   Madrid   Munich   Paris
Hong Kong   Singapore   Tokyo   Cape Town   Sydney

Editor in Chief: *Karen Hanson*
Series Editor: *Patricia Quinlin*
Series Editorial Assistant: *Annemarie Kennedy*
Marketing Manager: *Taryn Wahlquist*
Production Administrator: *Anna Socrates*
Editorial-Production Service: *Matrix Productions*
Electronic Composition: *Publishers' Design and Production Services, Inc.*
Composition Buyer: *Linda Cox*
Manufacturing Buyer: *Andrew Turso*
Cover Administrator: *Linda Knowles*

For related titles and support materials, visit our online catalog at www.ablongman.com

Between the time Website information is gathered and then published, it is not unusual for some sites to have closed. Also, the transcription of URLs can result in unintended typographical errors. The publisher would appreciate notification where these errors occur so that they may be corrected in subsequent editions.

Library of Congress Cataloging-in-Publication Data

Rae, Ann.
  Changing agency policy : an incremental approach / Ann Rae, Wanda Nicholas-Wolosuk,
    p. cm.
  Includes bibliographical references and index.
  ISBN 0-321-05491-1
    1. Social service—Government policy. 2. Social service—Planning. 3. Social work
administration—Planning. I. Nicholas-Wolosuk, Wanda. II. Title.

HV70.R34 2002
361.6′0973—dc21   2002024885

Printed in the United States of America

10   9   8   7   6   5   4   3   2   1   06   05   04   03   02

Contents

Foreword

Changing Agency Policy: An Incremental Approach by Ann Rae and Wanda Nicholas-Wolosuk is a wonderful book for social workers in any type of practice. There are several outstanding elements that I would like to call to the reader's attention. First, the overall focus on agency policy is something that is long overdue. Historically, social workers have tended to focus on the individual and family ("retail" social work) on the one hand or "macro" big picture, state or national social policy ("wholesale" social work) on the other. We have missed, I think, an important middle area—what the *agency* does or does not do, will or will not support. The agency is the work environment for much of what happens in social work, whether it be a private or a public agency (although these distinctions are becoming increasingly blurred today). While there are areas of social work/social welfare that agency policy cannot address, there are many to which agency policy is central. Consider policy about clients, for example. Caseloads are governed by agency policy. The number of visits/interviews available to clients are agency policy. Sometimes the matters are small. For example, I once saw an agency, housed in an old home on a now-busy street, that had a few parking places in front of the building. There was a big sign against the back wall which said "NO CLIENTS!" I was never sure where they were supposed to park. There are many other examples, but suffice it to say that agency policy is crucial to client well-being.

Another vital area of policy has to do with the treatment of the workers themselves. Consider, for one example, the fact that social work salaries are far from what they should be in agencies. Compensation policy is agency policy, and better compensation will not result from anything but changes in agency policy. Again, many other examples could be given, but the point is made. Agency policy is central to the social work enterprise. For this reason, calling our attention to the importance of agency policy is exactly right.

This book does more than point to an important area, however. It is also a call to action for social workers to look at agency policy as something that might be inadequate and that can be changed. All too often, in my experience, social workers accept agency policy as a "given," an acceptance, I might add, that agency executives frequently encourage. As one who works in the management area myself, in teaching and practice, I welcome this systematic focus on agency policy.

Of major importance—the authors give a model for changing agency policy: the Action–Strategy Model. It is a wonderful guide for workers who may not feel comfortable, or as comfortable, using social work to change agency policy because they may not feel they understand the steps involved. While all change processes have, essentially, a similar set of steps, we are often more comfortable applying them to known arenas of practice rather than new ones. This Action–Strategy Model should be a great help.

The Action–Strategy Model begins in exactly the right place—"Dream About Policy Change." All change processes must have a dream. Without it, there would be nothing to inspirit and inspire us. We may not achieve our dream in its entirety, but all change starts with hope. This book gets it right.

On a more practical level, the book is very manageable, with a wonderful summary section at the end of each chapter, along with learning exercises and study questions. It is very well written, and easy to use and apply. Students and professors will find it a joy.

John E. Tropman, Ph.D.
The School of Social Work
University of Michigan
Ann Arbor, Michigan

Preface

There is a rapid and ever-increasing devolution of social welfare policy between federal and state decision-making bodies and local and community agencies. The traditional social welfare system that began during the administrations of Franklin D. Roosevelt is being dismantled, and large pieces of the social welfare delivery system and "safety net" programs are being scattered to distant corners of the republic. Who will pick up the pieces?

Probably not social workers. Why not? Are not social workers totally committed to protecting those members of our society who suffer from poverty, discrimination, and social injustice?

Social work is based on four tenets: (1) its professional values, (2) its Code of Ethics, (3) the "person in the environment" concept, and (4) service to those who are in need of protection due to discrimination and social injustice. Social work practice, however, sometimes appears quite different. Perhaps this is because of the pervasiveness of the market-model approach or perhaps it is because of the submission to managed care decrees in the current practice field, both of which are often detrimental to clients/consumers. Regardless, the gap between social policy and social work practice is widening.

Social workers want "to help people," and "do therapy," and they assume that organizations, programs, funding resources, and policies will be in place that will allow this to occur. Despite the well-recognized body of literature and research about social welfare policy and the practice of community organization, intervention in the environments of organizations and communities has been sadly neglected in social work practice.

We have observed over the past decade that social work students do not seem as interested in learning about social welfare policy in general, nor do they seem to realize that it can be a specific type of social work practice intervention that can be carried out by direct-services staff. Therefore, *Changing Agency Policy: An Incremental Approach* contains a policy practice model that includes a series of specific steps that can be used by social workers to affect change in agency policy. And our observations—drawn from years of classroom discussions, volunteer activities, and field placement internships—have shown us that once students discover that they can actually bring about incremental change in agency policy, they become excited and gain confidence in their ability to apply theoretical knowledge to practice situations.

Our broad but feasible purpose, then, is to teach students that relevant change in social welfare agency policy can be achieved by social workers in their own agencies, especially when they have a stake in bringing about change needed to benefit clients/consumers. We think that it is possible for social work practice to be directed toward changing social welfare agency policy *and* to be carried out within the framework, values, and Code of Ethics of the profession. To achieve this purpose, we introduce The Action–Strategy Model of Agency Policy Change, which is *prescriptive* in nature and sets forth a deliberate course of action that can be carried out by social workers. The Model is focused on the change process from the point of recognizing that change is needed, up to the point of implementing the necessary change. It is particularly useful for students and social workers who wish to move beyond analyzing policy and to develop skills to impact policy for change.

There are several reasons for the approach we suggest. We maintain the focus on the development and implementation of a plan of action for convincing decision makers to approve implementation of a proposed change, because we believe that more emphasis is needed on teaching students skills required to be effective in the crucial phase of policy change: convincing others and gaining necessary approval. While only a small number of social work students and social workers will find themselves involved in analyzing and evaluating policy in their careers, many will have opportunities to be involved in a change effort in some way. Our goal then, is to give them skills with which they can avail themselves of those opportunities in an effective manner.

Change is afoot. The perception of social workers as "bleeding hearts"and "knee-jerk liberals" is slowly fading away as they begin to manifest characteristics that combine "soft-hearted" with "hard-headed" approaches in their interventions (Gibbs, 1991). The infusion of the scientific method and emphasis on the development of critical thinking skills in social work curricula, as mandated by the Council on Social Work Education *Educational Policy and Accreditation Standards* (effective July 1, 2002), represent a step in the right direction for the profession. This text clearly demonstrates that if social workers want to survive in the twenty-first century, they must learn to incorporate social welfare policy practice interventions, and to ground those approaches in the scientific method as an integral part of their professional repertoire.

Material in the text is alive and timely—a dull and boring social welfare policy textbook will not benefit the inquisitive social work student who most likely has a preconceived idea that learning about social welfare policy is dull and boring. To command the attention of the student, the chapters are developed around questions and activities that increase understanding and ability to develop an agency change approach through application of various parts of the Action–Strategy Model. Case examples affecting organizational change are also presented.

Having said that, we need to point out that the model proposed in this text begins with a stage we refer to as the "dream." Why the word "dream"? Are we suggesting that social workers need to spend more time in mental meandering or recreation and relaxation? While that is sometimes needed, this is not the meaning of the word "dream" that we are suggesting. According to *The American Heritage Dictionary of the English Language* (Pickett, 2000), to dream can mean many things, such as, "a daydream; a reverie . . . a condition or achievement that is longed for; an aspiration . . . To regard something as feasible or practical . . . to conceive of, imagine." As we use "dream" in this book, it should be interpreted as "the ability to see potential for improvement in a situation." This kind of dreaming leads to the development of ideas and sometimes then to development of a plan for action. The proposed model then leads the social worker to move from a "dream stage" and its resulting ideas, into planning and action.

Chapter Summaries

Chapter 1—Social Work, Social Change, and Policy
Practice in the Agency and Community
Information in Chapter 1 includes a discussion about why social work is chosen as a professional career. Reasons why social workers need to understand social welfare policy and where they need to practice it are explored, and the authors' definition of agency policy is set forth. Concepts of organization theory including climate and culture, the community and community organization practice, are introduced to explain why social workers need this knowledge to practice in these environments. A key term, "Solution-Based Incrementalism," is introduced as it serves as the underlying theme that permeates the presentation of ideas throughout the text.

Chapter 2—The Social Work Theory Base of Agency Policy Intervention
This chapter examines the role of social work theory as it pertains to social work practice and changing agency policy. Issues of social change, social control, value conflicts, and the sanctions of intervention in organizations and communities to change agency policy are addressed as they impact social work practice.

Chapter 3—The Action–Strategy Model of Agency
Policy Change: Foundation and Overview
A foundation of the Action–Strategy Model is presented, which includes six principles to assist social workers with the theory and knowledge required before attempting an agency policy change. A case example that illustrates an agency policy change situation in a human service organization is described. A brief overview and outline of the Model and its four Components are also set forth in this chapter.

Chapter 4—Explanation and Application of the Model: Components I and II
Components I and II of the Model, Dream About Agency Policy Change and Analyze the Policy Situation Related to the Change Idea, respectively, are delineated in Chapter 4. Content provides guidelines to help social workers gain insight and knowledge about initiating, analyzing, and formulating a hypothesis for an agency

policy change that results in benefits for clients and consumers. Action steps in these Components that pertain to the case example in Chapter 3 are discussed.

Chapter 5—Explanation and Application of the Model: Component III

Information in Chapter 5 explores the step-by-step process contained in Component III of the Action–Strategy Model, Develop a Plan of Action Related to the Change Goal/Idea, which progresses from dream to reality to a goal statement about the agency policy change. Further, it is demonstrated how social workers can move the goal forward by selecting a change strategy that impacts the development of a plan for implementation, evaluation, and stabilization of the change effort. Content is also linked to the case example in Chapter 3. The usefulness of the Model for social work practice is discussed in light of a strengths perspective that draws on assets of social workers and consumers of their services.

Chapter 6—Explanation and Application of the Model: Component IV

Chapter 6 focuses on the fourth and final Component of the Model, Implement the Change Strategy to Accomplish Approval of the Agency Policy Change. Guidelines and suggestions are set forth that can be used by social workers as they take deliberate action steps to execute a change strategy. Presented are techniques and skills associated with proposal writing, oral presentations, and the use of electronic technology that assist social workers to persuade decision makers to affect agency policy change. Ideas from the case example in Chapter 3 are also examined.

Chapter 7—Values, Interests, and Diversity in Human Service Agencies

The role that values play in planning for the development and implementation of agency policy change is explored in Chapter 7. Material about the changing environment of social work practice and the need for social work intervention in the policy area to reflect different approaches to meet the needs of diverse populations, women, and people of color is also presented. The concept of cultural competence in social work practice is explored and a new term, "diversity competence," is introduced and discussed in light of social work practice and agency policy change.

Chapter 8—Agency Policy Change, the Practice of Social Welfare Policy, and Social Work in the Twenty-First Century

A case example that illustrates how social workers can use aspects of the Action–Strategy Model to bring about policy change in larger systems is presented. The devolution of social services programs and the shift in responsibilities for the administration and implementation of these programs from national and state levels to community organizations and the implications for social work practice are explored. Advanced are ten principles for social workers to consider when bringing about transformations in social welfare in political and economic environments at the federal, state, and community levels. Future directions for the profession of social work and social welfare policy interventions are also presented.

Audience

The primary audience for this text is college students in BSW and MSW programs in the United States and other countries. Social work field placement directors and instructors in BSW and MSW programs will also find this text useful for the step-by-step guidelines for bringing about incremental change in agency policy. The text is also relevant for students in political science, psychology, sociology, and applied sociology courses at the undergraduate level as well as nursing, public administration, and organizational behavior courses at the undergraduate and graduate levels. Instructors in internship programs in these disciplines will also be interested in this text as a tool to enhance learning experiences in student practicums.

Assessment of student learning outcomes in regard to the material presented in the text during the past sixteen years in the classroom confirms that the step-by-step change process contained in the Action–Strategy Model of Agency Policy Change is realistically applied to policy situations in human service organizations. Students are highly motivated to learn how this approach can be used as a guide to "practice policy."

A secondary audience for this text is professional social workers and middle management administrators who are employed in community social welfare agencies in the United States.

Teaching Tips

Each chapter in the text is introduced with a goal statement and concluded with a list of important terms that have been defined and discussed in the chapter. The textual discussions are augmented by the use of examples, study questions and learning exercises designed to teach specific skills including policy situation analysis, agency assessment, proposal writing, position papers, and oral presentations to decision-making groups.

About the Authors

Ann Rae

Ann Rae, Ph.D., ACSW, is Professor Emerita of Social Work at Saginaw Valley State University, where she taught for twenty years in the social welfare policy and research methods curricula. Professor Rae also served as the Chairperson and Field Placement Coordinator of the Social Work Program at Saginaw Valley State University. She has also been a faculty associate in the School of Social Work at Michigan State University in the MSW Distance Education Program and in the School of Social Work at Arizona State University, Tucson Component. Dr. Rae holds a

Bachelor of Arts degree in American Studies from Dominican University (formerly Rosary College) in River Forest, Illinois, a Master of Social Work degree in the policy, planning, and administration sequence from Western Michigan University in Kalamazoo, Michigan, and a Ph.D. in Higher Adult and Continuing Education from the University of Michigan, Ann Arbor. Prior to her academic experience, she was employed in several human service organizations, including the Cook County Department of Public Aid in Chicago, Illinois, the Michigan Department of Social Services (now the Family Independence Agency), the State of Michigan Office of Services to the Aging, and community-based family service agencies. Professor Rae has presented papers and scholarly research at national and international social work conferences on several topics, including adult protective services, continuing professional social work education, the role of evaluation research for social workers, the practice of social welfare policy, and the importance of electronic technology for social workers.

Wanda Nicholas-Wolosuk

Wanda Nicholas-Wolosuk, ACSW, is an Adjunct Professor of Social Work at The University of Michigan–Flint. She has also been an Adjunct Professor of Social Work at Saginaw Valley State University, where she taught social welfare policy and child welfare courses for the past sixteen years. She holds a Bachelor of Arts degree in Psychology/Sociology from The University of Michigan–Flint, and a Master of Social Work degree from The University of Michigan, Ann Arbor. Professor Wolosuk has served as the Field Placement Coordinator of the Social Work Program at The University of Michigan–Flint, as well as teaching policy classes. Concurrent with her academic experience, until 1996, she was employed in several human service organizations providing child welfare services. Those organizations included the Michigan Department of Social Services (now the Family Independence Agency) Child Welfare Licensing Division, Saginaw County Child Receiving Home as the agency director, and Genesee County Consortium on Child Abuse and Neglect. Professor Wolosuk has presented workshops at state and national conferences on such topics as child abuse and neglect, child welfare licensing issues, foster parent training, the practice of social welfare policy, and development of community collaborative efforts.

We introduce this text with confidence that it will serve the profession by providing a format for the development of social work practice skills in the area of social welfare policy and a formula for a timely change model of intervention in human service agencies.

Ann Rae
Wanda Nicholas-Wolosuk

Acknowledgments

We express our thanks and appreciation to the many people who have assisted us and encouraged our efforts throughout the duration of our writing effort. In the initial stages of the writing, there were many questions to be answered and Dr. Ronald C. Federico provided support and guidance, and was always willing to listen to our concerns, answer questions, and provide insightful comments. Professor Roland L. Warren provided a sounding board for early drafts of the text and offered suggestions and alternative ways of approaching various concepts that helped us to clarify critical topics and details. We thank Professor Warren for his lifelong contribution to the fields of social welfare and social change theory and appreciate his wisdom and encouragement.

At Saginaw Valley State University, many persons assisted with activities that affected our on-going effort, including faculty colleagues in the Department of Social Work: Nellie Monroe, Steve Yanca, Robin McKinney, and Judy Berglund; Dr. Donald J. Bachand, Dean of the College of Arts and Behavioral Sciences; Pat M. Latty and Vivian K. Wressell, Faculty Secretaries; Anita Dey, Head of Library Reference; Scott Mellendorf, Reference Internet Librarian; John Mauch and Cheryl Burtrum, Reference Librarians; and, Brian Mudd and Kirker Kranz of the Library Audio/Visual Unit.

A special word of appreciation is extended to Leah Segura, BSW, who served as our research assistant throughout the process. Her patience and willingness to carry through regardless of the tasks at hand were exemplary.

H. James Geistman, Jr., Lecturer of English at Saginaw Valley State University, also provided valuable assistance by editing major sections of the text. He offered constructive criticism and suggestions that improved the overall direction of the language and content of the text material and we acknowledge his contribution.

Debbie Gerardo, Field Placement Instructor for university social work students, provided insights about the content on social work contracts and we appreciate her time and efforts.

Saun L. Strobel, Technical Publications Secretary at Saginaw Valley State University, typed the entire text. We are forever in her debt for her proficiency and professionalism in working with us in an objective and level-headed manner while managing to keep her sense of humor throughout the process. She also provided us with moral support when it appeared as if the end of the project would never come. Her efforts greatly facilitated the completion of the text.

At the University of Michigan, Flint, Department of Social Work, we thank Professor Charles Bailey, Chairperson of the Social Work Department, and Professors Everett Blakely, Charles Jones and Kathleen Woehrle for their enthusiasm, encouragement, and on-going support of this effort.

We extend special thanks to Dr. John E. Tropman, Professor of Social Work and Nonprofit Management, School of Social Work at the University of Michigan, Ann Arbor. He was extremely helpful in regard to providing information about social welfare policy, change strategies, and models of social change, as well as assisting with analyzing major portions of the text. We appreciate his effort and encouragement.

We also thank Janice Wiggins of Addison Wesley Longman, who initially reviewed our proposal and initiated the contract to publish the text. Her words of support were especially reassuring during the early days of the project. When the social work text publishing unit at Longman was transferred to Allyn and Bacon, Ms. Wiggins provided a smooth transition to that company where Judy Fifer, Senior Series Editor, and later, Patricia Quinlin, and Karen L. Hanson, Editor-in-Chief, Social Sciences, effectively assumed responsibility for the completion of the book. We are also grateful to the following reviewers for their helpful comments: Ed Gumz, Loyola University Chicago; Mark Hanna, California State University Fresno; Fay Wilson Hobbs, University of Alabama; Carolyn Jenkins, Xavier University; Michael Evan Johnson, Tuskegee University; Dr. C. G. Kledaras, Campbell University; and Nancy Mary, California State University San Bernadino.

We also recognize the social work students in the social work program at Saginaw Valley State University for completing a summary survey in regard to the content of the text and its value for social work practitioners. Without their support, our book, *Changing Agency Policy: An Incremental Approach*, would not have been finalized.

Our daughters and sons, granddaughters and grandsons, and great-grandsons provided warm words of support throughout the process, and we thank them for their patience and love.

Ann Rae especially thanks her wonderful husband, John, for his unyielding support and eternal encouragement to finish the text. Without his love and exhortation, the book would not have been completed.

Wanda Nicholas-Wolosuk especially thanks her daughter-in-law, Gail, for her willingness to take over the major responsibility for running the horse farm. Without her hard work, time to work on the book would not have been possible.

Finally, our hats are off to social workers throughout the world who have the courage, dedication, and persistence to fight against poverty, discrimination, and social injustice. Their contributions to the well-being of humankind are recognized and admired.

Social Work, Social Change, and Policy Practice in the Agency and Community

Goal Statement

To develop an awareness of why social workers need to understand social welfare policy and where they need to practice it.

Discussion

Massive changes in America's social welfare system have occurred since Ronald Reagan became president in 1980. The population has grown older and is living longer. A conservative political and economic agenda is very much in evidence; witness the *devolution* or transference of power and responsibilities for social welfare policies by the federal government to local government and community decision-making organizations. This process continues to invidiously affect the design of policies and programs administered by community agencies.

As a result of this, questions have arisen regarding how the social work profession will handle the current situation. Are social workers more concerned with maintaining the status quo of the present day, adapting to managed care and privatization practices, buying into the current political and economic agenda, and accepting the fact that there is very little that can be done to deal with what has become known as the "permanent underclass"? Have we accepted the market model approach to social welfare? Where will social workers function, given the present political climate of devolution, declining resources, managed care, and privatization of social welfare services?

Onward to the private sector. The private sector, whether it be nonprofit or proprietary, depends on the initiation of public social welfare policy and the continuation of tax dollars for its livelihood. The question becomes, "Who will ensure that public funds are appropriated and allocated to human service agencies?" Master of Business Administration (MBA) graduates? Industrial Biology graduates? There is no escaping the importance of social welfare policy. If you want to work as a social work practitioner, then you must come to grips with the idea that, whether you like it or not, you will be impacted by social welfare policy.

What About You?

Regardless of where social workers practice or are employed, they need to understand how social welfare policy is analyzed and undergoes change. Social workers can impact the policy process at the social welfare agency level so that their role is an active one, one that shapes social change to benefit and empower clients/consumers of social services. Reflecting the idea of Alfred Kahn (1973), who stated that all practice follows policy, it is fitting that social workers understand what social welfare policy consists of and that social work practice can be directed toward changing agency policy.

When you considered social work as a course of study, did you think that "practice follows policy?" Did it ever enter your head that social workers were in any way remotely connected to the social policy process, or did you simply picture yourself in an agency office or in the home of a client/consumer, developing a relationship and interacting in a one-on-one situation? Let us spend a few minutes engaging in a brief exploration about your reasons for selecting social work as your career choice and whether or not you think there is a connection between social work, social work practice, and social welfare policy.

What Are Your Reasons for Choosing Social Work as Your Course of Study and Career?

Social work students and practitioners, when asked about their reasons for choosing social work as a course of study or career, typically respond that they want "to help people" and "become a therapist." Students rarely state that they are desirous of intervening in the social welfare policy process. A study by Hanson and McCullagh examined motivational factors present in the choice of social work as a career. Hanson and McCullagh ranked twelve factors on a scale of 1 (lowest) to 10 (highest) as to why students chose social work as their career. While items such as "working with people" (overall mean score of 9.35) and "contributing to individuals" (overall mean score of 9.03) ranked highest on the survey, the factor entitled "effecting social change," was also given favorable placement in the questionnaire results with an overall mean score of 8.61. The authors found that students ranked highest those items in the category of "service to others" and that students choose social work for "altruistic" reasons, such as "working with people, contributing to individuals and society, believing that they could succeed in the profession, and effecting social change as important factors" (Hanson & McCullagh, 1995, 28–37).

The respondents ranked in lower order survey items such as "job opportunities, working conditions, and salaries," summarized by the authors under the category of "job self-interest." Further analysis in this study revealed that the category of being of "importance to others" had decreased slightly during the past five years (prior to publication in 1995) without an accompanying increase in the "importance of job self-interest" category. This point is intriguing considering the low salaries earned by bachelor of social work and even master of social work graduates. It may suggest that social work students, while not totally uninterested in their working conditions, continue to be motivated more by factors associated with providing services to those in need.

Inherent in the act of "working with people" and "contributing to individuals" resides the social worker's belief that some type of change will occur in the life of the client/consumer; in addition, the social worker believes that his/her intervention will be a key reason as to why that change will occur. However, since the days of the Charity Organization Society and Settlement House Movement, social workers have taken on the dual responsibility of bringing about change in both interpersonal *and* environmental systems. This responsibility entailed working with the individual so he/she will change, working with the environment so it will change to benefit the individual, or working with both! This approach is known as the *Person-in-Environment Theory* or the *PIE Approach* (Karls & Wandrei, 1994). It directs the social worker to not only "start where the client is" but requires that the worker possess knowledge of larger issues—such as the conditions in the social, cultural, economic, and political community—that may affect the behavior of the client/consumer.

So it seems important, then, that social workers address what it is that makes them different from other professions that "help people." If "helping people" is truly what social workers desire, is not social change inherent in the process? We cannot continue to "fix people" in our agencies and then send them back into neighborhoods made up of gangs, illegal drugs, and unsafe housing. A way to begin this inquiry is to question how and in what way people can be helped and what role is played by social change in the helping process.

Think about it. What other profession claims social "change" as its essence? Do nurses, doctors, lawyers, teachers, or psychologists practice social change? Perhaps somewhat, but social change is not their primary focus. Lawyers may engage in the practice of social change by appealing decisions and establishing new legal precedents, but change is usually secondary to their oath of providing a total defense on behalf of their consumers and clients. Social change is a major focus of the social work profession alone, and social workers must examine ideas about the usefulness of social change for their clients/consumers. Only then can they understand the nature and uniqueness of their own professional destinies.

Social Change and the Profession of Social Work

Why do social workers need to know about the nature and process of social change at various societal levels? An important reason is that social workers do not practice in a vacuum—they function in a social, cultural, political, and economic world. It is useful, then, to have some explanation of social change to understand why events occur and issues emerge. These events and issues may cause economic hardship or social injustices that interfere with the ability of individuals to carry out activities of daily living in a satisfactory manner. These changes affect functioning at the agency level as they reverberate from larger to smaller systems.

Change is part of life, and many theorists—Parsons, Hauser, Coser, Kuhn, Simmel, Warren—have set forth various theories of social change such as conflict, psycho-social, equilibrium, and evolutionary. According to Johnson, Schwartz, and Tate (1997) *social change* is an "alteration, modification, or substitution in the institutions, structures, patterns of organizations, and exchanges and relationships between people in a given society." Social workers need to know all about such change. They "help people" with all types of changes that impact their lives. Sometimes, social workers "win a few"—they help a client/consumer adapt to a life change. Sometimes, social workers "lose a few"—they do not help a client/consumer adjust to a life situation. Sometimes, social workers not only "win a few," but they assist clients/consumers to redirect their behavior in a purposive manner. This type of change, purposive change, is the most satisfying and rewarding. Let us examine more concepts about the idea of purposive change.

Purposive Change

In 1977, in his text, *Social change and human purpose*, Roland Warren set forth a two-fold classification of social change. This discussion is still timely in the twenty-first century. Warren calls one type of social change *crescive* and the other *purposive*. *Crescive* change is "out there" and ongoing in the day-to-day, month-by-month, year-to-year activities of living. *Purposive* change, on the other hand, is distinguished as a deliberate intervention into an existing condition in order to achieve some objective. Purposive change will not occur unless someone wills it. The characteristics and properties of the entity that is to be changed will also be different than they were prior to the intervention (Warren, 1977). Social work practitioners, because of their education and training, are more interested in understanding the dynamics of purposive change—how they can change the course of events—rather than how different social changes come about. They are curious about "the relationship between the process of social change and the attempt to influence this process by deliberate intervention" (Warren, 1973). It is purposive change, then, that social workers must understand if they are indeed to understand "how and in what way people can be helped," and if they wish to affect change in agency policy.

Solution-Based Incrementalism and Purposive Change

Several years ago, one of the authors became engaged in a lengthy conversation with a State Representative and one of his aides. The conversation evolved into a discussion about a recent piece of legislation which represented a response to a major child welfare issue. During the conversation, the author made the remark that, while the legislation was a beginning, it was disappointing in that it fell far short of what was needed. The State Representative replied that legislation generally occurred in this way—in a piecemeal fashion. He agreed that the legislators could often ascertain the full scope of the problem, especially with the assistance of legislative aides who did extensive research for them on issues. He went on to say, however, that usually it was beyond feasibility for them to respond to the whole problem. Therefore, they usually chose a piece of the problem to respond to and, hopefully, continued that process with other pieces of the problem at later times. This is, of course, an incremental approach. The assumption on which this approach to legislative change is based is that once enough pieces of the problem are responded to, all of the responses together will represent a solution. The author's reaction to this explanation was to ask the question: "Do you also have a pretty good idea what the solution to the whole problem would be, or could you know through the same research?" The State Representative replied that he thought generally that was possible. The second question then asked was: "Would it not be better to decide what the total solution might be, and develop legislation which would represent pieces of the solution, rather than pieces of the problem?" While that legislator thought it was a marvelous idea, it has not become the usual way of doing business in legislative bodies. It seems obvious to all of us that responses to pieces of the problem have not accumulated into a solution for most of our social issues. So why not try the incremental approach from the framework of solutions rather than problems?

This approach is very similar to the *strengths perspective* which is now emphasized in social work. It requires social workers to focus attention on the positive aspects—those factors and characteristics on which they can build—in any given situation. It applies in working with groups, organizations, and communities as much as it does when working with individuals and families. When we look at a situation, we can either focus on the negative aspects of the situation (the problem), or we can look for solutions/strengths to improve the situation. While this might not appear to be a significant difference in approach, it actually is a subtle yet crucial shift in attitude and focus for purposive change. We might think of this approach as *Solution-Based Incrementalism*.

Direct Service Social Workers and Policy Practice

In later chapters we will again turn to a discussion of social change and social work practice. At this point, however, we want to introduce some ideas that are crucial for social workers when they attempt to bring about change in agency policy—the major focus of the content of this text. When social workers engage in this kind of intervention it is often referred to as *policy practice* or "professional efforts to influence the development, enactment, implementation, modification, or assessment of social policies primarily to ensure social justice, and equal access to basic social goods" (Barker, 1999). Social workers who are direct service workers can "practice policy." *Direct service workers*, sometimes referred to as front line workers, are those persons who assist client/consumers in "face-to-face" situations and help them to carry out their activities of daily living in an effective manner. Direct service workers can be BSW or MSW trained social workers. When engaging in policy practice at the agency level, direct service workers continue to provide services to clients/consumers, but also work with the procedures and policies of the agency system to make these more responsive to meet client needs. We now turn to a discussion of several key definitions that are necessary to understand for this kind of social work practice.

Agency Policy Defined

We offer a definition of *agency policy*, as follows:

> *Agency policy* consists of those principles and guidelines by which an agency through its programs and services carries out its mission and goals. Agency policy may be formal and written or informal and unwritten, but it is commonly known by agency personnel, and it results in such things as procedures, forms, questionnaires, training packets, programs, services, projects, and electronic technology applications.

While agency mission statements and program goals and objectives are reflected in agency policy, and while program and job descriptions are reflective of policy, they are not agency policy in and of themselves. Neither are laws which affect the agency, although they are often the motivation for specific procedural policies.

Our definition of agency policy departs from the idea that an agency policy has to be written and passed on by a legitimate authority such as an agency Board of Directors. The rationale for this is based on our observations of the manner in which agency staff carry out daily activities and the way in which patterns of work behavior become the norm for completing required tasks despite the fact that the "norm" has not been developed in written form or found in a procedural or operations manual. Informal policies are often found in the informal structure of the agency. According to Horejsi and Garthwait, the

> term *informal structure* refers to various networks of employees and unofficial channels of communication based mostly on friendships and personal associations. This informal structure is sometimes cynically described by staff as "the way the agency really works." It becomes apparent only after working in the agency for an extended period of time (Horejsi & Garthwait, 1999).

For example, when workers spend a day in the field making visits to the homes or living arrangements of their clients/consumers, it may or may not be customary to provide an itinerary for their supervisors of those visits, complete with addresses and telephone numbers. The worker may simply say to the supervisor, "Well, I am going out in the field to visit clients to complete quarterly reviews. See you tomorrow." The obvious reason for the provision of a list of visitations would be one of concern for the safety and the ability to contact the worker if an emergency situation should arise. While it would be helpful for agency staff to have such a written policy formally stated in an operations manual, many organizations have not developed these type of procedures. Perhaps workers in a specific agency provide a list of field visitations for their supervisor regardless of the fact that there is no written policy. In these dangerous days, and, based on the necessity for taking extra precautions for safety reasons in many human service agencies, it would be beneficial if this type of unwritten practice could be developed into an agency policy with a formal, written status.

Examples of Agency-Level Policy and State-, Federal-, and National-Level Policies

Agency-Level Policy	State-, Federal-, and National-Level Policies
Creation of a standard referral procedure to public housing units for physically and mentally challenged clients/consumers in a community advocacy agency for disabled citizens	Creation of a proposal to amend the Civil Rights Act of 1964 as amended in 1968 prohibiting discrimination in housing
Revision of child care provisions at a domestic violence shelter for mothers who are victims of physical abuse	Expansion of the Child Care and Development Block Grant of 1990 to address needs of children in domestic violence centers
Creation of a Women, Infant and Children's (WIC) outreach policy in rural counties by a regional public health department	Creation of additional eligibility requirements for applicants of the federal WIC Program at the county level
Creation of a uniform drug testing policy for recovering addicts in a residential substance abuse treatment agency	Development of state confidentiality protection laws for persons with substance abuse problems who participate in the Medicaid Program
Revision of a bereavement education policy for family members in a hospice agency, which includes confidentiality protections	Expansion of Medicare rules and regulations to require mandatory attendance by family members in bereavement programs in all hospice organizations

(continued)

Agency-Level Policy	State-, Federal-, and National-Level Policies
Completion of a funding proposal for a job training policy regarding resume writing and employment interviews for low-income adults in a public assistance agency	Creation of additional work and training regulations for low-income families who participate in a county Temporary Assistance to Needy Families Program (TANF)
Development of a pregnancy prevention policy for adolescents in a community family service agency	Creation of a program change in the Adolescent Pregnancy Prevention Program of the Children's Defense Fund

As you can see from the examples in this table, our focus on agency policy is concerned with the day-to-day procedures and activities carried out by direct service providers within the local agency environment. Agency policy is within the realm of immediate control by direct services workers.

The Action–Strategy Model of Agency Policy Change Defined

Let us now turn the discussion in this chapter to a definition of the Action–Strategy Model.

> The *Action–Strategy Model of Agency Policy Change* is a professional, change-based intervention at the agency level. It includes a role for clients/consumers, incorporates *critical thinking* (application of the steps in the scientific method) and the values and Code of Ethics of social work, and is intentionally directed toward a segment of society that will benefit from its effects.

Application of the Model can be thought of as embarking on a journey of change with positive experiences occurring at the end of each component. An overview of the Model and the four major components is presented in flow chart form in Figure 1.1. The Model is discussed in detail in Chapters 4, 5, and 6.

The Action–Strategy Model

FIGURE 1.1

What Do Social Workers Need to Know Prior to the Application of the Model?

Because the Model focuses on changing agency policy, social workers who decide to use it should know something about their agency and the community environment before engaging in a deliberate, purposive change process. Knowledge about agency and organizational settings is critical for social workers to understand before they apply the Model. These settings are now examined and discussed.

Human Service Agency Defined

According to Etzioni (1964), we are born, develop, mature, live, and die in organizations. The organization that is the natural habitat of social workers is known as the human service organization. Netting, Kettner, and McMurtry (1998), who draw on a definition originally set forth by Brager and Holloway (1978), define *human service organizations* as "the vast array of formal organizations that have as their stated purpose enhancement of the social, emotional, physical, and/or intellectual well-being of some component of the population." Human service organizations are also known as agencies and these terms are often used interchangeably (Flynn, 1985; Dolgoff, Feldstein, & Skolnik, 1997; Horejsi & Garthwait, 1999; Landon, 1999). A reason as to why social workers use these phrases to refer to the same thing can, perhaps, be traced to the early days of the profession when pioneer social workers established "voluntary agencies" in their respective communities. These agencies formed the bulwark of services in localities for many years prior to the entrance of federal, state, and local governments in the field of social welfare. An *agency* is "an organization that is authorized or sanctioned to act in the place of others. It performs activities that some larger group or organization desires and is willing to fund" (Horejsi & Garthwait, 1999).

Our definition of a human service agency is as follows:

> A *human service agency* or organization is a formal, living structure which has as its goal the provision and delivery of goods and services necessary to assist people to live in a decent manner so that their common human needs are met.

Types of Agencies.   *Public agencies* are created by statute and legislation promulgated by elected officials at all levels of government. A public school, a county medical care facility, a state department of public health, and the federal bureaucracy known as "Health and Human Services" in Washington, D.C., are examples of public agencies. *Private agencies* are divided into nonprofit organizations (voluntary agencies) and for-profit (proprietary agencies) and are found in numerous communities in America. Examples of nonprofit organizations are the community family and childrens' agencies and Lutheran and Jewish social services agencies. Many private, nonprofit agencies are funded in part by community United Way Planning Boards. Examples of for-profit agencies are child care organizations and substance abuse treatment and counseling centers.

Further, social workers can practice in *social work organizations*. These are classified as organizations whose primary goal and service is the provision of social services, such as child and family service agencies. Sometimes these agencies are referred to as *guest* settings. They are also employed in *host* organizations, where social work services are secondary to the dominant service, such as public schools, medical centers, and nursing homes. In addition, social workers may also practice in organizations that bring together several disciplines, one of which is social work, to meet the needs of specific client/consumer groups. These types of organizations are sometimes referred to as *midway* settings, such as an outpatient mental health center. These organizations may be public or private, and private organizations may be nonprofit or for-profit (Popple & Leighninger, 1996). These organizations are found at the national and federal levels, in state and regional settings, and in local communities. The majority of social workers are direct service workers who practice in nonprofit, community-based organizations.

The Formal Characteristics of Human Service Agencies and Organizations.   Included in the *formal* aspects are the mission statement, organizational chart, agency domain, goals, funding sources and financial considerations, and external relations, such as regulatory sources and effectiveness studies regarding programs. Social work students are often asked to analyze a human service agency in a social welfare policy or community organization course or during their field placement experience. This is usually viewed as a ho-hum assignment. It is an essential one, however, because students will eventually be social workers and they will learn that they must carry out responsibilities within a regulatory structure that governs and controls an agency that is set up to deliver social services to clients/consumers. This information becomes critical when planning to bring about change in an agency policy.

The Informal Characteristics of Human Service Agencies and Organizations.   The *informal* aspects of an agency are infinitely more interesting than an organizational chart or learning about the goals and objectives of an agency and its programs. Informal characteristics reflect the values, beliefs, feelings, emotions, and impressions of the staff. They are the conscience of the organization, the blood, sweat, and tears that are shed not only by the professional and technical support staff but by the clients/consumers who are served by those staff. As noted in the cartoon strip "Frank and Ernest," in which the cartoon characters are viewing an organizational chart, the question is asked: "Which do you think is more important, what you know or who you know?" with the answer as follows: "Neither. It's what you know about who" (Thaves, 1999).

Social work students are rarely asked to analyze the informal characteristics of an organization, even though they eventually realize as social workers that this aspect must oftentimes be negotiated, mediated, stroked—and sometimes ignored—before any client/consumer intervention can be undertaken. A social worker engaged in agency policy change must have knowledge about the informal aspects in her/his practice at the human service agency before undertaking an agency policy change. Knowledge of the formal and informal structures that operate within the agency, often the output of the organizational theory, are also critical to keep in mind when workers attempt to engage in purposive change efforts.

Organizational Theory in Human Service Organizations and Agencies.   If social workers engage in purposive change efforts they must also understand and become aware of some of the major organization theories that helped to shape the environment in which they are employed. According to Dessler (1980, 1986), these "theories help us to understand the structure and behavior of organizations, and to predict how a change—such as widening the span of control—may influence the structure, behavior, and effectiveness of the organization."

The Role of Organization Theory

Definitions of organization theory abound. One definition, however, offered by Dessler is simple and easy to understand, as follows: "Organization theory itself can be defined as the subject concerned with understanding, explaining and predicting how to best structure an organization to fulfill its goals" (Dessler, 1980, 1986). Further, Dessler comments that Freud set forth a theory of human behavior and what type of treatment to use, and that organization theory "serves about the same purpose in management. By consolidating what we have learned from observing organizations, organizational experts have developed a set of rules (or a *theory*) that can help managers reorganize their companies effectively."

The terms "organization theory" and "management theories" are often used interchangeably. They are frequently discussed in historical sequence dating from the Egyptians and Greeks forward. A way to group organization theories is also offered by Gary Dessler (1980, 1986). He divides them into "classical organization theories" dating from pre-industrial times to shortly after WWI and "contemporary organization theories" ranging from the 1920s to the present day. In a similar fashion, Kettner, Daley, and Nichols in their text, *Initiating change in organizations and communities: A macro practice model* (1985), introduce Weiner's classification of organization theory into "traditional theories such as bureaucratic, scientific management, administrative management, human relations, systems, structural functionalism, organizational psychology, and sociotechnical systems."

In their text, *Social work macro practice*, Netting et al. (1998) explore the literature about various organizational theories. They develop information about these into "*descriptive*" and "*prescriptive*" categories and state that "descriptive approaches are intended to provide a means of analyzing organizations in terms of certain characteristics or procedures" and "prescriptive approaches are designed specifically as 'how-to' guides, [in order] to help build better organizations." Further, it is stated that prescriptive organization theories include treatises on management and leadership. In addition, Netting, Kettner, and McMurtry present information about "whether each particular theory approaches organizations as *open systems* or *closed systems*. Open-system perspectives are concerned with how organizations are influenced by interactions with their environments, while closed-system approaches are more concerned with internal structures and processes."

Hasenfeld discusses organizational theory as it affects administrative tasks in human service organizations in the text, *The Handbook of Social Welfare Management* (2000). He states that these organizations are different from other types of organizations because they "work on people to transform them" and that the technologies that are used by the staff are dependent on the "reactivity of the clients." In order to provide "service effectiveness," the staff in an agency (and in particular, the administration) look for guiding practice principles that are based on the choice of an "underlying organizational theory that offers a rationale for these principles." Various organizational theories including rational-legal, human relations, feminist perspective, contingency, Neo-Marxist and radical feminism are assessed by Hasenfeld in terms of applicability for practice in social welfare administration. The discussion is summarized by suggesting that many organizational theories lack validity especially for use in human service organizations. It is further pointed out that social welfare types should not be tempted to adopt "popular management models that lack empirical validity or sensitivity to the attributes of human service organizations" (Hasenfeld, 2000). The idea is set forth that while social welfare administration needs to be aware of the role played by organizational theories, they also need to "embrace and adapt organizational theories that most effectively address its particular administrative issues within the social welfare context."

There is an abundance of texts and publications about organization and management theories for the social welfare administrator who may be a social worker. Direct service staff, who may also be social workers, need to be knowledgeable about the theory or theories that best characterize their agency as this will guide them when planning to change an agency policy. For example, it is more difficult to bring about agency policy change in an organization that is grounded in bureaucratic theory as the lines of communication and worker responsibility are well defined and specific and a line worker will not have a great deal of freedom to make changes. Often, the behavior of staff which operates in the informal structure of the organization is dependent on the culture and climate of the organization. Therefore, direct service workers must also be aware of two more components of the agency environment: organizational climate and culture.

Organizational Climate and Culture

The phrase, "organizational climate," has been discussed for a longer period in social science research and literature dating back to the 1950s when compared to the term, "organizational culture," which began to emerge in the late seventies (Glisson, 2000). Often these phrases are used interchangeably, but differences between the two phrases began to appear in scholarly works and journals in the 1990s. Some definitions have been set forth and are briefly presented here.

Organizational Climate.   *Organizational climate* is described as the "feeling that one gets while working somewhere. Like the weather, that feeling can be warm and hospitable; it can also be cold and hostile" (Weinbach, 1998). Some of the attributes of a favorable organization climate are teamwork, mutual respect and confidence, understanding of respective roles, advocacy, maximum autonomy, good communication, and feedback to managers (Weinbach, 1998). It seems that these attributes are dependent on the quality of leadership that exists in an agency or human service organization. If an organizational climate is healthy and the leadership robust, it is likely that the agency will meet its goals of serving clients in an efficient and effective manner. Glisson defines organizational climate as a "property of the individual (perception) that is shared by other individuals in the same work environment. That is, organizational climate is the shared perceptions that employees have of the psychological impact that their work environment has on those who work there" (Glisson, 2000).

Organizational Culture.   *Organizational culture* is defined as a "property of the collective social system. It comprises the norms and values of that social system that drive the way things are done in organizations including those that are for-profit, nonprofit, public, and private. These norms include how employees interact, how they approach their work, and what work behaviors are emphasized in the organization through rewards and sanctions" (Glisson, 2000). Organizational culture for social workers refers to the values that are internalized and used as a guide for action by them to provide effective services for clients/consumers. The overall guiding principles for social workers are, of course, the six core values of the profession and the National Association of Social Workers Code of Ethics.

It is important to keep in mind the distinction between *corporate culture* and *organizational culture*. Corporate America has been exposed to numerous treatises about the culture of organizations for the past several decades, such as those advanced by Ouchi (1993, 1981), Peters and Waterman in their book *In Search of Excellence* (1982), W. Edwards Deming, the creator of Total Quality Management movement (1986) and Socio-Technical Systems (STS) (1988). These approaches stress greater cooperation and communication between administration and workers wherein managers rely on staff to work jointly with them to initiate change and create new policies. According to Fisher and Karger (1997) the "STS approach is based on the belief that attention must be paid to both the technical and social aspects of production" and "if workers are able to interact in the course of their work and have their needs addressed, they will be happier and more productive." The term organizational culture is often used interchangeably with *corporate culture*, which reflects ideas about how values and beliefs affect workforce output in for-profit organizations. For example, the STS approach reflects production tactics of the "much-publicized Volvo plant in Udvalla, Sweden, where teams of six to eight workers built complete cars" (Fisher & Karger, 1997). The definition of corporate culture is very similar to the concept of organizational culture but it reflects ideas about how values and beliefs affect workforce output in for-profit organizations. It is also a multi-dimensional concept that is dependent on leadership, trust between employees and administrators, the strategies and vision of the organization. It too consists of the central norms, customs, and values that characterize the organizations as a whole. It may be viewed as a positive or negative attribute that influences the performance and success (or lack thereof) of the organization. Corporate culture can shape the behavior of individuals and groups through a system of rewards and approvals so that there is compliance with the purpose of the organization. In short, corporate culture is a way of doing things in an organization that is so ingrained in the psyche of its members that they do not consciously think about or question the way they behave, carry out, and complete activities or tasks, all of which are directed toward making a profit for the corporation. We might also hasten to add that many ideas about *corporate culture* that have been advanced during the past 25 years relate to ways that production can be increased in manufacturing and the durable goods sectors of the economy, and not in the realm of human service organizations. The question remains, what can social workers find that is useful in these theories that will benefit the delivery of human services to those in need of assistance, which is a markedly different process than building automobiles.

Glisson sums up the distinction between climate and culture by remarking that "culture captures patterns of social interaction, and climate captures the personal meaning that individual workers give to those interactions" (Glisson in Patti, 2000).

Implications for Social Workers Who Plan to Bring about Agency Policy Change. Why are the concepts of organizational climate and culture important to social workers when planning to bring about change in agency policy? The attainment of agency goals and the effective delivery of services to clients are dependent on the "relationships and interactions between service providers and service recipients" (Glisson, 2000). The delivery of service often rests on the type of organizational climate and culture that permeates the organizational environment. Similarly, the implementation of a plan to change a policy is dependent on the interactions between direct service workers, middle management, higher administration, and the clients/consumers.

One might expect that human service organizations, which play such a vital role in our society, would be fixtures in our communities. Unfortunately, many public human service and nonprofit agencies are disappearing from the social welfare landscape. Some reasons for this are increasing competition for decreasing resources, block grants that states implement with few restrictions imposed by the federal government, and managed care approaches that require professional staff to provide credentialing, specified treatment protocols, and outcome evaluation studies or risk the loss of reimbursement from third-party providers. Social workers need to understand the importance of formal and informal agency structure, organization theory, and organizational climate and culture of human service organizations and agencies if they wish to continue to provide services for those who are in need of assistance.

We now turn our attention to some ideas about the community and its importance to the practice of social work and agency policy change.

The Role of the Community

Just as there are numerous definitions of human service organizations, definitions of the community are equally abundant. Social workers must have a basic understanding and knowledge of the communities in which they work in order to practice effectively.

The classic definition of the term *community* in the social science literature is set forth by Warren (1972) as "that combination of social units and systems that perform the major social functions" to assist people in carrying out the activities of daily living.

Warren also delineates five functions of the community that are carried out by its members in their day-to-day living activities as follows: (1) production, distribution, consumption to meet the basic needs of obtaining food, shelter, and clothing; (2) socialization to reflect the norms and values of the community; (3) social control to make certain that norms and values are internalized in the behavior of community members and the institutions in which activities are performed; (4) social participation to enhance interaction and relationships among community members; and, (5) mutual support to help one's neighbor in times of need and emergencies (Warren, 1977). When there is a breakdown in any or several of these functions, human service organizations need to be in place to help people through periods of distress and crises to prevent further problems from occurring. These functions are carried out in varying degrees depending on the make-up and type of community in which one resides.

Types of Communities.   The *triple community* concept (Cox, Erlich, Rothman, & Tropman, 1979) includes a description of the types of community as a geographical or territorial unit, or a mixture of cultural and subcultural groupings, or a "mind-set" such as the academic or social work practice community. In their text, *Social Work Macro Practice* (1998), Netting, Kettner, and McMurtry draw on the work of Felin, who further refines earlier ideas of theoretical community types set forth by Tropman and Cox.

The *geographical, spacial,* or *territorial perspective* examines ways in which a community meets the needs of its residents and how neighborhoods and barrios, for example, also are called communities that are smaller in nature and which are distinguished by specific identities.

The *non-place perspective* or "communities of identification and interest" are non-geographic and are composed of "functional communities." People are drawn to this type of association based on their values, ethnicity, or interest in an issue of social, economic, or political concern. A "chat room" on the Internet or world wide web could be considered a "non-place community" as people communicate from around the world on an issue or topic that is of interest to them in some form.

The *personal networks or individual's membership in multiple community perspective* is similar to a layering of affiliations and relationships. For example, many of us belong to professional organizations, live in neighborhoods, and communicate with a myriad of other people via e-mail, chat rooms, and face-to-face interactions.

The Formal Characteristics of a Community.   The *formal* elements of a community include demographic information such as population statistics, occupational levels and health data, and geographic boundaries. Information about community institutions such as churches, schools, government, and news publications are included as part of the formal structure of most communities. Data about these variables are gathered by students in social welfare policy or community organization courses to help them learn about the major characteristics of the community in which they will execute their field placements and possibly secure employment. While these data are important, they hold meager value for students and social workers unless they relate it to the dynamics of the community, its informal structure, and the human service organization in which they practice.

The Informal Characteristics of a Community.   *Informal* elements of a community include the significant types of social groupings that exist, such as the religious, political, racial, social class, and cultural and subcultural units. What do people like most or least about their community? What makes the community a good or bad place to live? Also examined in the community are those institutions that have the greatest power and influence, the position of human service organizations and the profession of social work, the levels of communication and major values, and beliefs of the citizenry. Social workers need to learn about community dynamics as they begin to identify forces that create, maintain, resist, or interfere in the agency policy change process. Simply stated, agencies exist in communities and their formal and informal characteristics affect agency policy and the practice of social work.

Community Organization Practice

Social workers impact and are influenced by the community every day of their working lives. In order to intervene in a situation that is causing some problem in their community, they must be knowledgeable about the definitions and various types of communities as well as the formal and informal characteristics that are in operation. Several theorists have developed practice approaches for use by social workers that are useful for community interventions. Historically, these include, but are certainly not limited to, the Settlement House Movement as epitomized by Jane Addams, John Dewey, and Lilian Wald, who intervened to educate community members for participation in the democratic process, and Eduard Lindeman's small group approach during the early part of the twentieth century; Arthur Dunham's agency-based model of organization in 1972; and, Kramer and Specht's grassroots community development and social planning combination tactics in 1986 (Fisher & Karger, 1997).

While Rothman initially set forth three approaches of community organization practice, he later added a fourth intervention modality that social workers can include in their practice. The theoretical approaches or "ideal" types are known as locality development, social planning, social action, and social reform.

According to Rothman, *locality development*, or Model A, refers to "community change pursued optimally through broad participation of a wide spectrum of people at the local community level in goal determination action" (Cox et al., 1979). A current example of locality development is the citizen movement to eradicate crack houses and street drug dealers—the "let's take back our neighborhood" type of effort.

Model B, also known as *Social Planning*, "emphasizes a technical process of problem solving with regard to substantive social problems, such as delinquency, housing, and mental health" (Cox et al., 1979). This approach is organized and coordinated by a social worker who collaborates with other interested persons in a rational process to bring about social change. A current example of social planning is a county-wide human service council headed by a social worker and charged with the responsibility of allocating Work First, Work and Training Funds to local service providers for education and day care services for families involved in the Temporary Assistance to Needy Families (TANF) program.

Model C, the *Social Action* approach, "presupposes a disadvantaged segment of the population that needs to be organized, perhaps in alliance with others, in order to make adequate demands on the larger community for increased resources or treatment more in accordance with social justice of democracy." Current examples of this approach would be the Gay Rights Movement and the Association of Retarded Citizens.

Model D, or *Social Reform*, is very similar to social action, Model C, because it also focuses on societal change. It is, however, change that is initiated by those outside the intended beneficiaries of the change. There is a defined role for an organizer in this model. The organizer comes from outside of the group that is attempting to bring about change. This idea is similar to that of the Settlement House Workers Movement in which the "betters" helped the "lessers" to improve their neighborhoods and social institutions. The social reform approach is ideologically motivated rather than laced with analysis and rational planning techniques (Kettner, Daley, & Nichols, 1985).

While Models A, C, and D focus on broad-based social change, Model B, social planning, is most closely associated with the functions of social work practice of community organization set forth by the National Association of Social Workers: policy analysis, planning, policy development, reviewing, and policy advocacy (NASW, 1981).

In 1995, Robert Barker in *The Social Work Dictionary*, set forth a definition of community organization practice as follows:

> The practice of community organization is defined as an intervention process used by social workers and other professionals to help individuals, groups, and collectives of people with common interests or from the same geographic areas to deal with social problems to enhance social well-being through planned collective action (Barker, 1995, p. 69).

The term *community practice* is important in this discussion about the evolution of community organization interventions. According to Weil, "*community practice* is a broad-based term that encompasses the processes, methods, and practice skills of organizing, planning, development and change" (Weil, 1996). She further states that

> organizing relates to bringing people together for the betterment of social conditions and for social justice in neighborhoods, communities, regions, nations, and the world. Planning involves a range of processes and technical methods from neighborhood service planning through interorganizational planning for service integration and resource allocation, to social policy planning and implementation from local to global levels. Development refers to the social, economic and sustainable development efforts to improve the conditions of life and protect the environment particularly for vulnerable communities and populations in poverty. Change refers to social action and social change strategies ranging from educational campaigns, to coalitions focused on strengthening services or changing policy, to social movements to redress social injustice (Weil, 1996).

Weil and Gamble provided a conceptualization of community practice (Weil, 1996) based on their research and field testing over several years. They set forth eight models that guide social work practice. The models are entitled: Neighborhood and Community Organizing; Organizing Functional Communities; Community, Social and Economic Development; Social Planning; Program Development and Community Liaison; Political and Social Action; Coalitions; and, Social Movements. Their work is presented in-depth in *The Encyclopedia of Social Work* (19th edition), as well as in an article in September of 1996 entitled, "Community building: Building community practice" in the journal *Social Work*.

Briefly speaking and for purposes of this text, the models of Weil and Gamble can be correlated with the practice skills or organizing, planning, development and change, mentioned previously in the definition of "community practice." The first practice skill is *organizing* and contains two models: Neighborhood and Community Organizing, which is particularly useful at the grassroots level. The second practice skill, that of *planning* is associated with the models of Program Development and Community Liaison and Social Planning and is targeted to the "perspectives of community and human services leaders, program funders and beneficiaries of agency services" (Weil & Gamble, 1995). The third practice skill is *development* and encompasses the model of Community, Social and Economic Development and is aimed at financial institutions and prominent members of a community. The fourth practice skill of *change* includes the models of Political and Social Action, Coalitions, and Social Movements. Targets of change range from the local community to national and federal levels and include the general public, elected officials, and government entities (Weil & Gamble, 1995).

Weil relates that the models in this framework can be viewed from a theoretical perspective as discrete in nature. In reality, however, they can be developed in a sequential fashion or even combined in groups of two or three depending on the change issue. This is similar to the "mixing and phasing" process adopted in the late 1990s by Rothman and Tropman regarding their approaches to community organization practice. It behooves direct service practitioners, middle level managers and agency administrators to be aware of these various models of community organization practice as they seek improvement of programs in their own organizations, link with consumers and clients and collaborate with various human service agencies and citizen groups throughout the community.

The Rediscovery of Community

According to Lawrence Martin in a selection entitled "The environmental context of social welfare administration" (Patti, 2000), there is a renewed interest in the community not only in American but worldwide. There are many reasons for this, but three critical reasons, Martin continues, are "the decline in public funding for social welfare, the reassessment of the role of social welfare professionals, and the rebirth of spirituality."

Declining public funding has resulted in local agencies devising new ways to deal with social problems. The role of nonprofit organizations has increased in importance in many local areas. Privatization has forced many of these to examine their traditional ways of service delivery. Sometimes this has led to these agencies closing their doors, especially when for-profit human service organizations can demonstrate that they can provide services more efficiently and effectively. Sometimes it has resulted in the redefinition of agency mission statements and creative financial arrangements leading to the initiation of new policies and programs. The second reason for the rediscovery of community is that social welfare professionals are realizing that they must form coalitions with other networks, both formal in nature—such as teachers, medical staff and law enforcement, for example—and informal such as the family and churches. Teamwork and collaboration among professional groups is the preferred way of tackling problems in today's communities. A strengths-based perspective that emphasizes the importance of human capital and asset building is widely accepted as community members attempt to discover solutions to longstanding concerns that have not been alleviated by federal and state policies. A third reason as set forth by Martin is the rebirth of spirituality wherein many "faith-based groups constitute an important component of social capital and are becoming increasingly involved in social change initiatives and the actual delivery of social welfare services" (Martin in Patti, 2000).

Implications for Social Workers Who Plan to Bring about Agency Policy Change.
Community organization as a practice intervention is important for social workers because human service organizations exist in communities—the agency in the environment concept! In fact, the phrase "task environment" is often used to describe the relationship of the employment agency to other community organizations. It is defined as those "external organizations on which an organization depends, either as providers of needed input (money, raw materials, client referrals) or as consumers of its output" (Netting, Kettner, & McMurtry, 1998). Social workers must work to make not only their own organization but other agencies responsive to the needs of

client/consumers. They must know to what agencies to refer clients when their employing organization cannot provide the desired service. They must also know who to contact when making those referrals, and that means learning about the politics and personal relationships involved in service delivery. If no service exists and there seems to be a need for it, then social workers must possess skills to create that service or perhaps develop a new program, or even a new agency. Social workers must be aware of the characteristics of the existing community delivery system and where it needs to be strengthened, including the positive attributes of their own organization.

Interagency Coordination and Collaboration.   Interagency coordination and collaboration in human services delivery systems has been discussed in social work texts and articles for many years. Neugeboren, in the text *Organization, Policy and Practice in the Human Services*, draws on the earlier writing of William Reid (1964) and defines interorganizational coordination as the "voluntary exchange between two or more autonomous agencies of complementary resources needed to achieve shared goals." In this definition the idea of coordination is a specific type of collaboration. Neugeboren further elaborates by discussing four characteristics of coordination wherein agencies collaborate and work together to achieve change: 1) "voluntary participation"—agencies have a choice as to whether they become involved with a change issue or effort; 2) "agency autonomy"—agencies remain independent and function in their own right yet can become involved with a change effort with other agencies; 3) "shared goals"—agencies may adopt similar broad goals such as protection or independence, yet set forth or retain their own distinctive policies and programs to meet those goals as related to the change effort; 4) "complementary resources"—agencies may share building space and receive monies from the same foundation or United Way Planning Board to address the change issue. Perhaps the least obtrusive yet most efficient manner for coordinating and collaborating across the organizational spectrum is through value agreement and consensus on an issue or situation in the community. When agencies voluntarily agree to use their assets and talents to create opportunities for positive change that address a particular issue, the barriers of competition for economic resources and control of services are reduced. The ability to develop collaborative relationships that cut across community groups will stand social workers in the twenty–first century in good stead as they plan to change agency policy whether that be from within or outside of their own organizations.

Summary

If the profession of social work is to survive in the next century, then social workers need to accept the fact that social work practice that brings about change in agency policy is as necessary as intervention with individuals, groups, and families. A revolution in the policy about the delivery of social welfare programs and services is upon us, and there are few human service groups that stand in the way of this revolution.

Social movements that resulted in public policy change in the 1930s through the mid–1970s were the exception rather than the rule in the history of social welfare in the United States. If all practice follows policy, as Kahn noted more than a quarter century ago, what in the world are we waiting for? Have social workers become less influential at the federal level? Is there a "policy practice drift" (Tropman, 1999) in social work that may lead to a policy crisis? Do we need to explore new political avenues that will place more of us at the table of decision making as members of our profession were represented decades ago? The answers may be too frightening to think about, but the profession needs to strongly generate responses so that it will not risk losing advances that it has fought for so vehemently in the past. It is more difficult for the rank-and-file members of the profession to directly effect and control changes in social welfare policy at the federal and state legislative and bureaucratic levels. We are not suggesting the abandonment of these fronts and are confident that social workers will continue to participate in various types of political activities ranging from voting to providing testimony at public hearings to joining demonstrations to protest a social injustice.

But there is one place where social workers are found, day in and day out, from 9:00 a.m. to 5:00 p.m. It is a place where they can still, if they so desire, exert direct influence—the "home front," a.k.a., the agency. But, why does it matter whether social workers affect change at the agency policy level? In essence, we may be asking workers to change policy that may make it harder on themselves. For openers, however, when change is not initiated in this setting, social workers find themselves in a default position in which they are merely instructed to execute policies coming down from "on high." As a worker in a human service agency, do you want to merely react to that type of change, or is it possible to discover ways to make those policies more humane and beneficial for the clients/consumers whom you serve?

Another important consideration is that the profession of social work is coming under greater scrutiny regarding the effectiveness of its services. There is competition at the local level for funds from public and philanthropic organizations. There is competition for third-party providers and clients/consumers who pay fees for services rendered. Social workers who initiate change in agency policy are attempting to provide the means by which clients/consumers will benefit from the results of those services. Agency policy holds workers accountable for their interventions. If we wish to continue to serve poor and vulnerable persons and families in their environments where they carry out their daily activities in an effective and timely manner, it certainly is our responsibility, it seems, to have a hand in the creation, implementation, and evaluation of those policies. Even though change involves risk, new growth for the profession can occur if there is a rebirth of advocacy and planning for vulnerable populations that is tempered with excitement, creativity, and critical thinking.

Important Terms and Phrases

Action–Strategy Model of Agency Policy
   Change
Agency
Agency policy
Closed systems
Community
Community organization practice
Community practice
Corporate culture
Crescive change
Critical thinking
Descriptive organization theory
Devolution
Direct and indirect interventions
Direct service worker
Formal agency aspects
Formal elements of community
Geographic community
Guest setting
Host organization
Human service organization and agency
Informal agency aspects
Informal elements of community

Informal structure
Locality development
Midway setting
Non-place perspective community
Open systems
Organizational climate
Organizational culture
Person-in-the-environment
Personal network community perspective
Policy practice
Prescriptive organization theory
Private agency
Public agency
Purposive change
Social action
Social change
Social planning
Social reform
Social work organization
Solution-based incrementalism
Strengths perspective
Task environment
Triple community concept

Learning Exercises

1. Use the questionnaire based on the ideas developed by Hanson and McCullagh (1995) to determine your reasons for choosing social work as your career. Use a statistical spreadsheet program such as MINITAB (McKenzie, Jr. & Goldman, 1999) or EXCEL (Boyce, 1997) to compute the results. How did responses in your group compare with the student responses as noted in the Hanson and McCullagh study as presented in Table 1.1? Discuss the results in your class relative to your ideas about social work, social welfare, and social welfare policy, and whether or not you think that you will be able to "effect change" when you become employed in a human service organization.

TABLE 1.1 Student Ratings of 12 Factors Related to Career Choice of Social Work, by Year

Importance of:	1983	1984	1985	1986	1987	1988	1989	1990	1991	1992	Overall Mean
Working with People	9.51	9.73	9.41	9.49	9.45	9.12	9.34	9.36	9.18	8.90	9.35
Contributing to Individuals	9.08	9.39	9.06	9.43	9.32	9.16	8.80	9.17	8.80	8.51	9.08
Contributing to Society	8.95	9.24	8.95	9.28	9.07	8.91	8.77	8.89	8.86	8.54	8.95
Believing in Own Success in Social Work	8.56	9.26	8.68	8.58	8.93	8.44	8.46	8.50	8.48	8.06	8.61
Effecting Social Change	8.56	8.83	8.41	8.68	8.72	8.60	8.39	8.81	8.11	8.18	8.53
Social Work as an Interesting and Challenging Career	8.70	8.60	8.40	8.59	8.58	8.21	8.20	7.97	8.26	7.10	8.26
Becoming a Better Person	7.90	8.10	7.61	7.89	7.23	7.18	6.65	6.80	6.37	7.23	7.31
Good Job Opportunities in Social Work	5.79	6.29	6.04	5.96	6.70	5.99	6.32	5.90	5.46	5.04	5.96
Job Security in Social Work	5.11	5.89	5.27	5.66	5.69	5.58	5.40	5.41	5.17	4.29	5.35
Good Working Conditions in Social Work	4.21	4.74	3.76	4.71	4.24	4.16	3.76	4.42	4.03	3.92	4.18
Status and Prestige of Social Work	3.84	3.81	3.16	3.85	3.28	3.87	3.05	3.36	3.86	3.66	3.56
Good Salaries in Social Work	3.33	3.58	3.22	3.16	3.10	3.45	2.89	3.01	2.77	3.27	3.18

Hanson, James G. and McCullagh, James G. *Journal of Social Work Education*, Vol. 31, No. 1 (Winter 1995), 32.

Questionnaire: Items Related to Choice of Social Work as a Career
Please rate the following questions on a scale of 1 to 10. Mark the number of your answer in the blank next to the question.

You chose social work as a career because of:

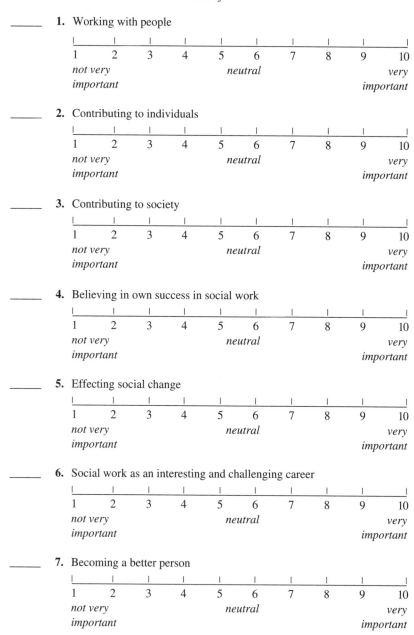

_____   **1.** Working with people

| 1 | 2 | 3 | 4 | 5 | 6 | 7 | 8 | 9 | 10 |

not very important   *neutral*   *very important*

_____   **2.** Contributing to individuals

| 1 | 2 | 3 | 4 | 5 | 6 | 7 | 8 | 9 | 10 |

not very important   *neutral*   *very important*

_____   **3.** Contributing to society

| 1 | 2 | 3 | 4 | 5 | 6 | 7 | 8 | 9 | 10 |

not very important   *neutral*   *very important*

_____   **4.** Believing in own success in social work

| 1 | 2 | 3 | 4 | 5 | 6 | 7 | 8 | 9 | 10 |

not very important   *neutral*   *very important*

_____   **5.** Effecting social change

| 1 | 2 | 3 | 4 | 5 | 6 | 7 | 8 | 9 | 10 |

not very important   *neutral*   *very important*

_____   **6.** Social work as an interesting and challenging career

| 1 | 2 | 3 | 4 | 5 | 6 | 7 | 8 | 9 | 10 |

not very important   *neutral*   *very important*

_____   **7.** Becoming a better person

| 1 | 2 | 3 | 4 | 5 | 6 | 7 | 8 | 9 | 10 |

not very important   *neutral*   *very important*

_____   **8.** Good job opportunities in social work

| 1 | 2 | 3 | 4 | 5 | 6 | 7 | 8 | 9 | 10 |

*not very
important*   *neutral*   *very
important*

_____   **9.** Job security in social work

| 1 | 2 | 3 | 4 | 5 | 6 | 7 | 8 | 9 | 10 |

*not very
important*   *neutral*   *very
important*

_____   **10.** Good working conditions in social work

| 1 | 2 | 3 | 4 | 5 | 6 | 7 | 8 | 9 | 10 |

*not very
important*   *neutral*   *very
important*

_____   **11.** Status and prestige in social work

| 1 | 2 | 3 | 4 | 5 | 6 | 7 | 8 | 9 | 10 |

*not very
important*   *neutral*   *very
important*

_____   **12.** Good salaries in social work

| 1 | 2 | 3 | 4 | 5 | 6 | 7 | 8 | 9 | 10 |

*not very
important*   *neutral*   *very
important*

Class Rank: Senior = 1; Junior = 2; Sophomore = 3; Freshman = 4

_____

Age:

_____

Sex: Male = 1; Female = 2

_____

2. Divide into groups of three. Members of each group should ideally live in the same community. Members of each group choose a human service agency in their local community and set up an interview with a social worker in the designated agency. Then, do the following during the interview:
   a. Review the definition of agency policy presented in Chapter 1 with an agency social worker. Ask him or her if the definition bears any similarity to what agency policy is in his/her organization.

b. Ask the designated social worker if there are differences in the definition of agency policy in the text relative to the definition of agency policy as found in his/her human service organization.

c. Take notes and report your findings to the class as a whole during the next session.

Study Questions _____

1. Why do social workers need to understand the concept of change?

2. Do social workers have a role in changing agency policy? Discuss your answer related to the concepts of agency policy.

3. Distinguish between guest and host settings for social workers.

4. Do you think that it is important to learn about some of the informal characteristics of a human service agency? Why or why not?

5. Some characteristics of formal agencies and organizations were set forth in this chapter in the section related to organizational structures. Can you think of additional characteristics of an agency that are important for social workers to know and understand? Why are they important? List and discuss.

6. Do social workers need to understand the agency and community settings when they are contemplating agency policy change? Why?

7. Why do social workers study and analyze the "community"?

8. Some characteristics of communities were set forth in this chapter in the section on formal and informal characteristics of a community. Can you think of additional properties of a community that are important for social workers to know and understand?

2

The Social Work Theory Base of Agency Policy Intervention

Goal Statement

To develop an awareness of the role that social control and social work theory play in policy intervention by social workers at the agency level.

Discussion

What Else Do Social Workers Need to Know Before They Apply the Action–Strategy Model of Agency Policy Change?

They Need to Know about Social Control and Values Conflict in Addition to Social Change. *All* social work professionals have the responsibility to initiate social change in human service agencies and communities if they discover some need that, if addressed, may be beneficial to their clients/consumers. Initiation of social change in agency policy, then, is not limited to staff in middle management and administrative positions. Social work students learn, according to the Council on Social Work Education Educational Policy and Accreditation Standards, that policy, or macro social work practice, is equally as important as practice with individuals and families or micro social work practice. For some reason, though, it does not appear that social work students and social workers have bought into this idea. Perhaps they have been reluctant to initiate agency and community change because it can be threatening and disruptive to their professional lives. We must ask ourselves, then, to what extent is it feasible to undertake change without risking one's credibility, position, and values? In order to answer this question we must examine issues involving (1) the social control of the change effort and (2) value conflicts, both personal and professional.

Social Control. What is *social control*? There are numerous definitions and discussions about social control in the social science literature. Social welfare policy, for example, is a form of social control as it provides for "the use of legal means to control the lives of people who are devalued by the larger society" (Johnson, Schwartz, & Tate, 1997). Social control may include a community function whereby groups influence member behavior to comply with group norms (Warren, 1972; Cox, Erlich, Rothman, & Tropman, 1984; Netting, Kettner, & McMurtry, 1993). Drucker (1974) refers to control as "direction" in that it "relates to an end stage, not the means; that it deals with expectations and with the future; that it is concerned with norms and with what ought to be."

Netting et al. (1998) note that "control implies an exercise of power" and if this *power* comes from outside the organization, such as a regulatory source, employees may be more likely to resist it. If the change comes from within the organization, employee resistance to it may be lessened. Regardless of the source of control, though, it is a given that agency control is required for staff to carry out responsibilities. How control is exercised by administration and staff is critical to social workers when they attempt to change agency policy. The smaller the change that the social worker is seeking and the greater the dissatisfaction with an existing policy, however, the greater the power and control the social worker will likely have regarding the policy to be changed (Warren, 1977).

Are Social Workers Wary of Social Control?

Who controls a human service agency or organization? The answer is: "It depends." The members of the Board of Directors, executive director, and middle management of a large, bureaucratic organization exert considerably more control regarding change than direct service workers or clients/consumers. Social workers have been cautious about the exercise of control in their employing agencies, most likely because their education emphasizes the importance of trust, self-determination, and autonomous functioning regarding human behavior. Direct service workers and middle management (a group that is consistently involved in a tug of war for control between the "top and the bottom"), however, may exercise more control in an open-systems type of organization wherein the lines of communication are open and flow more easily from "bottom to top" and vice-versa.

One reason that social workers may be wary of social control is that they are used to working with individuals and/or families rather than administering budgets, supervising programs, and devising mission statements. Social workers do exercise control over the activities of their clients/consumers and must be aware of this as it is easy to abuse the use of control. When social workers intentionally intervene in an existing situation on behalf of a client/consumer, however, they exert social control merely by the act of intervention. They exercise explicit or implicit control simply by virtue of occupying a professional position in an agency. If the change involves only one client/consumer or a family, workers and clients/consumers may be able to share control of the issue and provide a solution through a joint decision-making process.

This may explain to a certain extent the preoccupation of the social work profession with individual change methods or therapies. There is more opportunity for control in a smaller system such as that of an individual or family, but there is also the chance to exercise democratic participation between the worker and the client/consumer system, for example. The worker may be more comfortable and less conflicted when power and control are shared.

Social control elements also exist in the community and include political, economic, religious, social, and cultural norms and practices. When the social worker attempts to initiate change in a service delivery system or agency policy that affects clients/consumers in some segment of the community, the playing field increases in size and more conflict and discomfort may arise. Control of the process as viewed by the social worker is less certain than it is when working with one client/consumer or family. A larger playing field may be viewed as a scary place for the worker because of numerous influences and differences in opinions of those involved. Social workers exercise varying degrees of social control in their day-to-day practice. It may be easier for the worker to sit back and take things as they come rather than become actively involved and make an effort to tackle something less predictable, such as an agency policy change or a controversial issue in the community.

Why Not Relax and Enjoy Life? Who Needs Social Change, Social Control, and Values Conflict? Answer: Social Workers, of Course!

If you had your druthers, wouldn't you rather just sit back, relax, do your work, get your paycheck, come home, and kick off your shoes day after day? A nagging feeling in your gut continues, however. What about those clients/consumers of yours who live in dilapidated housing in sub-zero temperatures and can see no way of relocating? Do you think that because you are a social worker with a professional Code of Ethics and a set of values, that you *must* intervene in an existing situation if the needs of your clients/consumers are consistently ignored by your agency or other community organizations? Do you feel like your intervention may make a difference?

Or, do you think that the situation of your clients/consumers may improve if you do not intervene—that time will take care of things, perhaps? This syndrome is known as "time heals all wounds." Therein resides the potential *value conflict*, however. As a social worker, you know in your head and you feel in your heart that change is warranted. If you do not respond, if you do not hear the cry, then how do you account for your decision of "no intervention"? How do you handle this potential value conflict in a professional manner that will best serve the needs of your clients/consumers while balancing whatever degrees of power and social control may be present, if you decide to initiate the change process?

Further, social workers need to understand that some types of change may be beyond their immediate control. For example, it is not possible for social workers in a public assistance agency to change the asset and income levels for Medicaid eligibility in their agency. If this type of policy change were pursued, it would necessitate working outside of the employing agency on one's own time with coalitions of interested advocates, state and federal legislators, and numerous bureaucratic staff.

Social workers do need to understand, however, that it is possible to introduce changes that will improve the day-to-day life situation of clients/consumers in their agencies. An example of this type of change might involve offering a series of community education outreach programs about the Medicaid Program and the Medicaid Spend Down section of that law. Development and implementation of this type of intervention offered by agency staff would be possible to execute, develop, and it might reach consumers who thought they were not eligible for medical assistance. Does the social worker or direct services worker have the right to introduce this type of change in their organizations?

Who Says that Social Workers Have the Right to Intervene in the Change Process?

The problem of social control is one that social workers grapple with as they carry out their interventions. How much control can the social worker exert and what are the trade-offs involved when one begins to lose control? Is the theory of democratic participation at the community level of decision making, wherein control is spread evenly throughout the group, the most practical method one can use in accomplishing the job (Warren, 1977)?

The word *intervention* is an appropriate one when discussing control and the practice of social work. It means that a worker comes between the problem and the client/consumer system in a professional manner. The derivation of the term "intervention" is from the Latin, "inter" meaning "in between" and the verb, "venio," or "to come." Other terms in the social work literature that are similar in meaning to *intervention* are practice, method, therapy, and treatment. Intervention is defined as "anything a worker does to help a client achieve some goal" (Gibbs, 1991). Hence, social workers view their interventions from the perspective of democratic planning wherein the worker and client/consumer jointly identify strengths and needs, and agree to achieve appropriate goals.

The very act of "coming between," however, implies that ripples, or control ruffles, may appear in a client/consumer situation. There is, then, the perception of social control, even though, at the initiation point of the change process, the worker did not intend any. Of course, the amount of social control depends on the situations in which social workers find themselves. A worker delivering child protective services can potentially cause significantly more ripples during the initial intervention than, perhaps, the worker who is visiting an elderly home-bound client/consumer to provide nutrition services. In a less restrictive setting where the worker has been extended an invitation to participate, such as an exploratory session to educate a group about substance abuse, little or no control is required to accomplish the goal of providing basic information.

The right of social workers to intervene in human situations has been examined from historical, social, political, economic, and moral perspectives. Gibelman (1995) states that "social work's sanction comes from the society of which it is a part. This implies that society recognizes that there are disparities between 'what is' and 'what should be' and there is a need to rectify this condition." Social workers have a right to intervene in client/consumer situations as derived from their professional value base and the National Association of Social Workers' Code of Ethics. Their professional education and training received from social work programs and schools of social work at the undergraduate and graduate levels that are accredited by the Council on Social Work Education also provide them with the proper credentials. Sanctions needed for intervention include state licensing and certification laws and regulations, community approval from the court and legal system, mandates from federal and state public policies such as Medicare and Medicaid, and the private sector including United Way Planning Boards, insurance providers and managed care corporations.

Social workers balance the issue of social control with the "right to intervene" every working day—Monday through Friday and sometimes on weekends. It must be remembered that "the right to intervene" and making changes in the way other people lead their lives is an awesome responsibility and that many change efforts turn out to have unanticipated, harmful consequences or iatrogenic effects (Warren, 1977; Gibbs, 1991).

However, every time a person asks for guidance, every time a family applies for some type of social welfare benefit, every time a group seeks support to meet an unmet need or works to change some condition in a community or society that is socially unjust, there is a validation of social work's mandate not only to intervene, but to execute an intervention in a manner that is humane and effective in nature. Do you find it somewhat peculiar that this potential source of power is often overlooked by practicing social workers? Social workers in human service agencies nationwide who are searching for direction in an ever-changing world of social welfare policy need to exercise control and act on their values to continue the mission of the profession and assist those in need of service. In order to do this, we need to understand what it is that we do!

By the Way, What Is Social Work and Social Work Practice, Anyway? What "Do You Do when You Intervene"?

How does one define what is meant by social work and social work practice, especially since the areas of intervention seem boundless and may potentially reach into numerous segments of society?

In 1970, the National Association of Social Workers defined *social work* as "the professional activity of helping individuals, groups, or communities enhance or restore their capacity for social functioning and creating social conditions favorable to that goal." This definition was followed with a commentary about *social work practice*:

> Social work practice consists of the professional application of social work values, principles, and techniques to one or more of the following ends: helping people obtain tangible services; counseling and psychotherapy with individuals, families, and groups; helping communities or groups provide or improve social and health service; and

participate in legislative processes. The practice of social work requires knowledge of human development and behavior; of social, economic, and cultural institutions; and of the interaction of all of these factors.

In 1981, in NASW's *Standards for the classification of social work practice, social work practice* was defined as

> consisting of professionally responsible intervention to (1) enhance the developmental, problem-solving, and coping capacities of people; (2) promote the effective and humane operation of systems that provide resources and services to people; (3) link people with systems that provide them with resources, services, and opportunities; and (4) contribute to the development and improvement of social policy.

These definitions of social work and social work practice are widely accepted by social work educators and practitioners because they reflect the worker's dual responsibility to assist the "person" who is in need of services, as well as to undertake projects that shore up the social environment to ensure a decent level of human functioning. Building on these earlier definitions and reflecting the values of social work, six purposes of the social work profession were delineated by the Council on Social Work Education, Educational Policy and Accreditation Standards (effective July 2, 2002):

1. To enhance human well-being and alleviate poverty, oppression and other forms of social injustice.
2. To enhance the social functioning and interactions of individuals, families, groups, organizations, and communities by involving them in accomplishing goals, developing resources, and preventing and alleviating distress.
3. To formulate and implement social policies, services, and programs that meet basic human needs and support the development of human capacities.
4. To pursue policies, services, and resources through advocacy and social or political actions that promote social and economic justice.
5. To develop and use research, knowledge, and skills that advance social work practice.
6. To develop and apply practice in the context of diverse cultures.

The preceding definitions of social work, its purpose, and social work practice include the idea that interventions reflect "the development and testing of professional knowledge and skills relative to these purposes" (Barker, 1995). The definitions also incorporate the idea of a systematic approach to social work practice when defining social work as the "applied science of helping people achieve an effective level of psychosocial functioning and effecting societal changes to enhance the well-being of all people" (Gibelman, 1995). The latter statement implies that there is a causal relationship between the intervention of a social worker and the effects that occur as a result of that intervention. It also links an age-old idea that has often been used to describe social work as both a science and an art. Barker's definition of social work coupled with the Council on Social Work Education's recent statement about what constitutes the purpose of the social work profession conjures the thought that social workers must be "scientist practitioners" who possess not only the characteristics of warmth, empathy, understanding, and respect for consumers of their services, but who also demonstrate the ability to integrate the scientific method in their interventions to avoid harmful or iatrogenic effects in their clients/consumers (Gibbs, 1991).

Along with the idea that social workers can be viewed as "scientist practitioners" is the thought that when people "achieve an effective level of psychosocial functioning" that the social worker is acting as an "empowerment agent" who is focusing on the strengths of the client/consumer. Johnson et al. (1997) drawing from the ideas of Torre and Saleebey, state that "empowerment is a process through which people become strong enough to participate within, share control of, and influence events and institutions that affect their lives." Social workers, then, bring into play elements of social change, power, and control while balancing value conflicts connected to their employing agency, community, and with clients/consumers. They do this as change agents through practice interventions that are based on empathy, understanding, and the scientific method. Gibbs (1991) describes this kind of social worker as "soft hearted"—understanding, empathetic, warm, and caring—and, *also*, "hard headed"—objective, questioning, and impartial. The combination of these two attributes is unbeatable when social workers practice on behalf of clients/consumers. Add these attributes to the idea that social workers can change agency policy and watch the explosions take place!

What Is the Theoretical Base of Social Work Practice?

So far, we have discussed some reasons for your decision to become a social worker, the role that social change plays in social work practice and social welfare policy, the importance of knowledge about human service agencies and the community, social control and value conflicts, the right to intervene with clients/consumers, definitions of social work and social work practice, and "soft-hearted/hard-headed" social workers as agents of change. Our discussion now turns to some thoughts about the theoretical base of social work practice.

Social Systems Theory.   Social workers intervene at many levels of society: individual, family, group, organizational, community, and societal. These levels are frequently referred to as social systems because all are inhabited by human beings; composed of interacting and interdependent parts; defined by boundaries that identify them; and, potentially (and hopefully), exchanging energy or information with the social environment via the throughput, input, output, and feedback loop process. Social system levels can be arranged in a *hierarchical structure* ranging from the larger (societal) to smaller (individual) or vice-versa. The terms *micro, mezzo,* and *macro* are sometimes applied to these various system levels or targets of intervention in an attempt to further classify their properties. Macro means large and is a term social workers may have borrowed from the study of economics. Mezzo means middle or medium and is a term that is often used to describe a type of soprano. Micro means small, as in microscope. When these terms are employed in social work practice, however, micro systems refer to interventions with individuals and families; mezzo systems refer to interventions with groups and communities; and macro systems refer to activities with organizations and the larger society.

Another typology of the classification of system levels groups them according to *direct* and *indirect interventions.* Those levels dubbed *direct* consist of interaction with individuals, families, and groups; the worker here interacts with people in "face-to-face" situations. This concept was defined earlier in Chapter 1. The levels described as *indirect* consist of activities that affect an agency, community, or society; the worker here intervenes at the agency level. A social worker who works with groups of people in an agency or organization engages in indirect social work practice by attempting to change the agency or part of it. The idea is that the result of this effort will eventually benefit agency clients/consumers served by the organization (refer to Chart 2.1 for a diagram of these concepts). In Gibelman's book, *What social workers do* (1995), drawing on Barker in *The Social Work Dictionary* (1991), indirect social work practice consists of

> those professional social work activities, such as administration, research, policy development, and education, that do not involve immediate or personal contact with the clients being served. Indirect practice makes direct practice possible and more efficient; as such, it is considered essential and of equal importance to the mission of the profession.

The practices, methods, therapies, and interventions used by social workers to help individuals, families, and groups followed a general thought development process that included linear and circular pathways to find a solution to the problem or to assist clients/consumers to meet a need. According to Johnson et al. (1997), "assessing the person in the situation now involved understanding the relationship between individuals and environmental systems, and the problems of social functioning that arise out of that interaction." Such a *social systems theory* emphasized that *all* systems are goal-seeking with interdependent and interchangeable parts that thrive on feedback from the larger environment. What this meant was that now clients/consumers and social workers would proceed toward a goal together. Social systems theory, then, became the theoretical glue that bonded social work methods (casework, family therapy, group work, community organization) and social welfare policy, planning, and administration, to the mission and purpose of the profession, and the definitions of social work and social work practice.

A social systems approach requires a worker to break down the whole system into its respective parts. To accomplish this, both the worker and the client/consumer system work together in a step-by-step process to meet the needs of the client/consumer system. The worker begins with the identification of the client/consumer sys-

Social System Levels

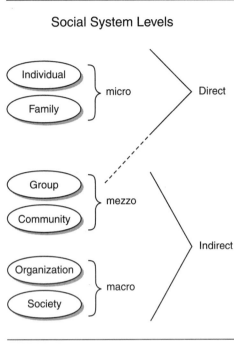

CHART 2.1

tem's needs and strengths and then continues with assessment, planning, and setting up goals and objectives. When these are completed, the plan (or alternative plan) is implemented, evaluated, and then the helping process is terminated. These steps appear to be linear in nature and imply a cause-and-effect relationship. But to think of them in this way would be misleading. In reality, the process used by the client/consumer and worker, in which they jointly examine information found in the environment, such as the community or place of employment, forces both worker and the client/consumer system to take into account the impact of the environment. Such a process, depending as it does on feedback from both the client/consumer system and environment, is most often nonlinear in nature.

Acceptance of the idea that human beings act differently in various environments forces the social worker to learn about human diversity based on culture, race, religion, gender, sexual orientation, and disability. These elements often combine in various ways throughout the step-by-step process of joint decision making. Inherent in systems theory is the concept that all systems are goal seeking so the worker and client/consumer collaborate to deliberately direct movement toward a desirable end. This developmental process may be completed in as little as one hour, or it may consume six months or a year of effort, depending on the type of goal that is identified and the "motivation, capacity and opportunity" (Ripple, 1964) that exist on the part of the worker and the client/consumer.

Social systems theory, however, is still evolving. Not only is the thought process utilized in interventions by social workers both linear and circular, but the systems being intervened in are more and more seen as nonlinear and complex. This has significance for practitioners engaged in purposeful change efforts, because traditional systems theory explains systems as stable, orderly, and rational, and emphasizes equifinality (the idea that systems starting at different states will still end up at the same state). Traditional system theory also emphasizes homeostasis and the role of negative feedback loops in inhibiting change (Warren, Franklin, & Streeter, 1998).

Some theorists now propose complex systems theory as a more current way of understanding systems. They describe systems as being path dependent, in that they are sensitive to initial differences or tend to amplify initial differences. This is referred to as multifinality in that two systems starting at the same state can develop in opposite directions because "small input can bring about large output if the input occurs at the right time and the right place" (Warren et al., 1998). According to Christopher Hudson in a recent article, this notion of sensitivity to initial conditions "originates in Lorenz's 1993 discovery concerning the unpredictability of weather patterns" (Hudson, 2000). He goes on to say that "small initial errors and perturbations sometimes endlessly magnify through positive feedback loops to create major changes, a phenomenon often observed in the physical sciences" (Hudson, 2000). The concept of multifinality is particularly relevant for a social worker contemplating a change effort. The implications are that "a single act of kindness or particularly well-timed intervention on the part of a social worker can have major repercussions." (Hudson, 2000). A social work practitioner then would need to do a very careful analysis of the agency/situation. A cursory overview that identifies factors common to most similar agencies would not be sufficient. For example, to identify the agency management structure, staffing patterns and requirements, budgeting process, for example, would not be an adequate analysis for change purposes. The social worker would also need to identify factors that are unique to this agency, such as the management style and level of staff empowerment, existing level of client involvement in agency decision making, special interests of Board members, and funding sources.

According to *complex theory*, systems also have a "degree of order that is as important as the potential or tendency for chaos" (change), and "are always changing from within" (Warren et al., 1998). This state of tension between order and chaos is described by some theorists as "the edge of chaos." The "edge of chaos" thinking resembles the idea that conflict is the normal state of affairs. In United States society, conflict is frequently seen as a negative condition, something to be avoided. However, conflict may also be seen as something inherent in everyday life. Dahrendorf might have predicted current thinking about complex systems theory and the nature of conflict in society, as follows:

> Every society is subjected at every moment to change; social change is ubiquitous.

Every society experiences at every moment social conflict; social conflict is ubiquitous.

Every element in a society contributes to its change (Appelbaum, 1970).

"From this point of view, social problems are the product of competition for scarce resources (wealth, prestige, power) which results in painful struggles over their distribution, with some being dissatisfied at the outcome." Further, "conflict theory assumes that values are held in common, that is, most people want the same things and will fight over their distribution." (Cox, Erlich, Rothman, & Tropman, 1987). Conflict, from this view, refers to the struggle for something that is scarce or perceived to be scarce (Johnson, 1992). It is seen as the impetus for all public policy as the government makes decisions regarding its role in relationship to the needs of its citizens (DiNitto, 2000). For purposes in this text, *conflict* may be defined as the condition in which there exists an opposition of alternatives, a condition in which more than one choice is possible. Life itself, then, may be seen as a series of conflicts. Conflict is neither positive nor negative, but its results may be—depending on the values that underlie the choices made during its resolution. Resolution of value conflict is more easily obtained in some societies than in others (Whitaker & Federico, 1997).

Roland Warren, in his early work on social change theory, referred to that state of tension that exists in systems, or the tendency toward change, when he defined crescive change as the change that is always occurring in social systems. He went on then to differentiate that kind of change from purposive change, which he defined as change that results from deliberate intervention in an already changing situation. While that idea has been around for a long time, it is still valid. What is different today is the rate of change. There is a lot of discussion currently about the interconnectedness of all countries and cultures—a world society concept. Systems theory, which explains how change in one part of a system affects all parts of the system, applies to systems at all levels; even worldwide. It has always been true that the actions of one country eventually will impact other countries. What has changed is how quickly the impact occurs and how quickly all are made aware of the actions and impact. With change at all levels occurring more and more rapidly, it is crucial that social workers engage in purposive change. In analyzing a system's readiness for change, practitioners should consider that the most adaptive systems are those maintaining enough order for continuity, while remaining open to change. They "exist in the center of a curve of flexibility" (Warren et al., 1998). A better understanding of systems theory and the change process from a nonlinear perspective, and recognition of human diversity and cultural differences will help practitioners avoid or decrease undesirable consequences of any change effort.

Social Work Practice and Agency Policy Change

When attempting agency policy change, the social worker engages in a deductive and objective reasoning process that eventually results in turning the question into an hypothesis that can be tested and measured throughout the application of a practice intervention. Next, the social worker uses all of the resources available in the agency and the community in a nonjudgmental manner to gather information, including listening to ideas expressed by clients/consumers who are in need of an agency policy intervention. We have observed, however, that social workers have only been paying lip service to the idea that clients/consumers should be brought along in the decision-making process throughout the intervention. In reality, it is not a common occurrence for clients/consumers to be involved in a change process that affects agency policy. This is unfortunate, because clients/consumers can bring special strengths to a change situation. The execution of an intervention should draw on the professional strengths of social workers and those of their clients/consumers in a positive and objective fashion. The idea that consumers and beneficiaries of the purposive change and the social worker have engaged in a joint decision-making process about whether or not an intended change will address the needs of clients/consumers in an appropriate manner links social systems theory and generalist social work practice. It also provides a way to integrate critical thinking with the "person in the environment" concept. It is an optimistic and upbeat approach.

Summary

All intervention levels in the hierarchy of social systems are affected by the initiation and implementation of social welfare policies. The generalist approach to social work practice reflects the idea that a social worker with a BSW is prepared for entry-level practice regardless of the level of intervention or complexity of the system. A social worker with an MSW and advanced generalist training possesses the knowledge and skills for intervention of all system levels, but with increased emphasis on assessment, planning, implementation, and evaluation functions with individuals, families, and organizations and in particular settings such as mental health or social welfare administration.

    While students at the undergraduate and graduate levels prepare for *generalist* (entry-level knowledge and skills for all systems levels) or *advanced generalist* (increased knowledge for more complex systems levels) practice, data based on survey responses of the membership of the National Association of Social Workers in the 1990s indicate that the majority of social workers stated that their primary function of practice was "clinical–direct service, and direct service was the modal response for BSW, MSW, and doctoral level members." Responses from members of NASW in the survey also reveal that social work macro-practice, that is intervention at the community and organizational levels, has been decreasing since 1988. It is also interesting to note that BSW graduates are more likely to engage in community organization practice functions when compared with MSW social workers based on the NASW survey (Gibelman & Schervish, 1993).

    It is expected that the majority of social workers engage in direct service to assist those clients/consumers who are in need. It is alarming, however, that there has been a large drop-off in the areas of community organization and policy intervention functions. Despite the fact that social work experienced a "clinical depression" (Gibelman, 1995) during the Reagan era, it seems that the profession of social work has gained wider public acceptance as the "helping profession" and the label of *"bleeding hearts"* (soft-hearted) and *"knee-jerk liberals"* (predictably liberal) is slowly giving way to the idea of the social worker as "scientist-practitioner." Despite such acceptance, there has been a redefinition of the social welfare system known as devolution. Witness the dismantling of the traditional "safety net" for the past twenty years, privatization, and the onslaught of the policy of managed care in the major fields of social work practice such as child welfare and mental health. Public sentiment supports the dismantling of the "safety net," but social workers continue to adopt a reactive rather than a pro-active stance to these recent changes. All the more reason for social workers at the agency level to use their theory and knowledge bases to intervene in policies in their organizations that are in need of change.

Important Terms and Phrases

Advanced generalist	Power
Complex systems theory	Social control
Conflict theory	Social systems levels of micro, mezzo,
Direct interventions	macro
Generalist	Social systems theory
Hierarchal structure of social systems	Social work
Indirect interventions	Social work practice
Intervention	Values conflict

Learning Exercises

1. Visit a human service organization where social workers are employed. Interview them about their responsibilities in the agency. Ask them if they view themselves as agents of social change and if agency policy assists them to empower clients/consumers whom they serve. Share your answers with your class.

2. You are a newly hired social worker in a human service organization that provides social services for recovering drug addicts. Several co-workers and you have recently become aware that there are no written safety and sanitation procedures for staff when testing urine for clients/consumers. The director of the agency is not concerned, stating that the county public health department team did not cite the agency for lack of an agency policy for this process. Yet, you are concerned about the safety of the clients/consumers with whom you work as well as yourself and co-workers. Would you feel comfortable about initiating change given this situation? If you decided to take action, what would be your first step? List and discuss.

Study Questions _____

1. Do direct service social workers have a right to intervene in an agency policy change process? Explain your response.

2. What effect does social control have on human service organizations?

3. How do the four purposes of social work, identified in this chapter, relate to the concept of social workers as both "soft hearted" and "hard headed"?

4. How does understanding social systems theory enable social workers to more effectively engage in a change effort?

5. Explain why the concept of multifinality is relevant to a social worker contemplating an agency policy change?

6. Should clients/consumers have a role in an agency policy change effort? Why? Why not?

3

The Action–Strategy Model of Agency Policy Change

Foundation and Overview

Goal Statement

To develop an awareness on the part of social workers that in addition to knowledge of the theory bases of organization and community, social systems and social work, the Action–Strategy Model of Agency Policy Change is built on a foundation of six star points that guide policy practice.

Discussion

Picture yourself as a social worker in an agency. You find yourself administering an agency policy that you think is unjust and discriminatory for clients/consumers whom you are attempting to help. Perhaps the situation is that there is no formal referral procedure for a prescription drug payment program for low-income seniors in your county commission on aging organization. Armed with your knowledge of theory and practice interventions, you are wondering if you would be able to change that situation. Perhaps you would like to standardize a referral process but know that you cannot accomplish this by yourself. You realize, however, that there is power in numbers. You know that you will have to enlist the support of your co-workers who have similar values and ethics and who are also interested in the situation. Before you initiate the steps in the Action–Strategy Model, it is necessary to examine the six star points that form its foundation.

Six Star Foundation Points of the Action–Strategy Model of Agency Policy Change

There are six star points or principles that form the foundation of the Model: Solution-Based Incrementalism; Bottom-Up Approach; Macro Social Work Practice for Direct Service Workers; Savvy Workers—Strong Clients/Consumers; Social Work Values and the Code of Ethics; and, A Systematic Process. It is recommended that social workers be mindful of these points so that they can incorporate this information in their practice repertoire prior to the application of the Action–Strategy Model. These concepts are now presented in the figure below and briefly discussed.

Point #1: Solution-Based Incrementalism.   You were introduced to this phrase in Chapter 1 in the segment about the conversation between one of the authors of the text and a state legislator. When social work students finish a volunteer placement or complete their first semester of field placement instruction in human service organizations, they usually learn that the change process in clients/consumers and agencies is incremental. They realize that there are situations in organizations that impede the application of the processes in theoretical practice models presented in class lectures. They discover that policy initiation and change often come about in a highly charged political and value-oriented environment. They realize that change is slow to happen and does not occur in an hour, a day, or a month. In the text, *Changing the System* (1981), Dluhy notes that an "'incremental' orientation toward change means that

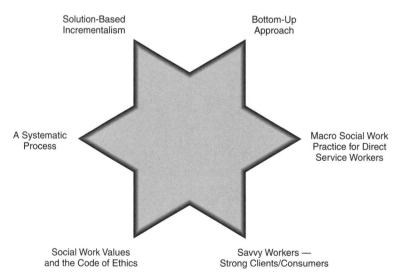

Six Star Points in Action–Strategy Model

Solution-Based Incrementalism

Bottom-Up Approach

A Systematic Process

Macro Social Work Practice for Direct Service Workers

Social Work Values and the Code of Ethics

Savvy Workers — Strong Clients/Consumers

FIGURE 3.1

while change at any one point in time appears small, if one looks cumulatively over a period of time, the changes begin to add up."

Incrementalism, humorously known as *"muddling through*," or the "sequential/ incremental model" was discussed by Braybrooke and Lindblom several decades ago. Lindblom, in an article in *Strategies of community organization* (Cox, Erlich, Rothman, & Tropman, 1970), remarks that "making policy is at best a very rough process." And further, "past sequences of policy steps have given him [the policy maker] knowledge about probable consequences of further steps." Lindblom continues,

> the policy maker need not attempt big jumps toward goals that would require predictions beyond his [hers] or anyone else's knowledge, because he [she] never expects the policy to be a final resolution of a problem. The change agent's decision is only one step, one that if successful can quickly be followed by another. Lastly, the policy maker often can remedy a past error fairly quickly—more quickly than if policy proceeded through more distinct steps widely spaced in time (Cox et al., 1970).

We have expanded the term *incrementalism* to include the phrase "solution-based incrementalism" as presented in Chapter 1. In this approach, social workers focus their attention on the positive aspects of a potential change situation—those factors and characteristics on which they can build in any given situation. They then seek solutions to improve the situation, all the while drawing on their own strengths and those of the allies and clients/consumers.

"Solution-based incrementalism" is not viewed as a widespread attack on the status quo. Let us learn from the mistakes of the Clinton health care reform movement of the early 1990s which reflected broad, sweeping changes and quickly went down to defeat. "Solution-based incrementalism" is also limited in scope to prevent worker burnout as it does not drag on forever and drag social workers down, as well. A modest agency policy change, for example, is easier for social workers to control. Solution-based incrementalism favors a cooperative and collaborative strategy in attempting agency policy change in keeping with the way that human service programs are successfully funded and operated in numerous communities these days. When we seek solutions we are given a chance to make some mistakes, sit back and assess the errors, and proceed in a correct manner. Learning from our errors is critical, however, as we initiate and develop change strategies for agency policy change. Social work students—simply recall the age-old fable of the race between the tortoise and the hare and welcome yourselves to the world of solution-based incrementalism!

Point #2: Bottom-Up Approach.   Society is made up of human beings, and, as such, it can be changed by them. What profession other than social work is better equipped to engage in change efforts to benefit those in need of services? Intentional, conscious, deliberate intervention to change a specific situation is the heart and soul, the science and the art, of social work practice.

Solution-based incremental change can involve a trained professional to lead and coordinate the change process. A great deal of the research literature tells us that most change initiated in agencies and communities starts from the administration at the top of the organizational chart and then filters to middle management and then to the line worker (Cox et al., 1970; Warren, 1977; Resnick & Patti, 1980; Williams & Huber, 1986; Griffin & Moorhead, 1986; Hall, 1991; Weinbach, 1998). The literature also contains information about how direct service workers can initiate change from a bottom-up perspective. It must be stressed, however, that the worker must be knowledgeable about the formal and informal aspects of the agency as well as its mission and purpose. The worker must also be viewed as credible in the eyes of the administration and his/her colleagues at all levels from the sanitation engineer (janitor), clerical staff, co-workers, middle management to the executive director. Perhaps best known in the human service management and administrative literature for a *"bottom-up"* approach are Rino Patti and Herman Resnick, who several decades ago set forth the idea that when direct service workers actively take on organizational change, they have the power to contribute to the overall effectiveness of the agency and its relationship with clients/consumers. Their ideas are worthy of review at this point. They discuss this approach as follows:

> To be sure, . . . involvement in change from below is the crucible on which organizational citizenship is forged. If human service professionals are to be more than mere technicians, they must concern themselves with the social issues that form the context of their work. Change from below is, if nothing else, a vehicle for enabling practitioners to see the important relationship between human service technology and social purpose (Resnick & Patti, 1980).

In the twenty-first century, the concept of a bottom-up approach wherein direct service or front-line workers attempt to influence and engage in agency policy change needs to be awarded greater credence than has previously been the case. The field of social welfare policy, whether it is housed at the federal, state, or local agency locations, is viewed as a practice domain wherein social workers regardless of their standing in the agency ply their trade to improve services for clients/consumers. They must make a commitment to attempt such action. True, the skills that are used by social workers at the various systems level will vary, but whatever the level of intervention may be, a social worker must always (1) analyze the need that is unmet, (2) join with others to attempt to remedy the situation, (3) plan in a rational manner to meet the need, (4) adopt a strategy of change to formulate the goals and objectives of the plan, (5) implement and evaluate the plan, and (6) eventually implement the change itself. Often, these activities are accompanied by the commitment that social workers carry out agency policy change *in addition* to fulfilling their responsibilities with clients/consumers. This type of activity falls into the practice repertoire of policy practice or macro social work practice as discussed further in the next foundation point.

Point #3: Macro Social Work Practice for Direct Service Workers.   Social welfare policy practice is often referred to as "macro" practice. According to Netting, Kettner, and McMurtry in their text, *Social Work Macro Practice* (1998), "macro practice is professionally directed intervention designed to bring about planned change in organizations and communities in internal and external environments, respectively. Any social worker regardless of levels of education and differences in agency or organizational settings can engage in macro social work practice." Earlier in the 1990s a comparison of policy–practice models was offered by Norman L. Wyers (1991). Wyers defines policy–practice as "a direct social work practice model with the potential to strengthen the social work profession's abilities to meet its century-long commitments of providing policy-informed services to those in need of them."

One of the models examined by Wyers (1991) is referred to as "the social worker as change agent in internal work environments" (or in his or her own agency). This model sets forth the idea that a direct services or front-line worker who thinks that an agency policy needs to be initiated, changed, or improved to enhance service delivery for clients/consumers should deliberately engage in that process. While the worker may be in competition or conflict with the Board of Directors, the administration, and some professional staff, he/she engages in a rational planning approach and selects a strategy to accomplish the desired organizational change (Wyers, 1991). The Action–Strategy Model incorporates this philosophy as it is aimed at changing agency policy rather than attempting change in larger systems such as state and federal social welfare systems as mentioned earlier. It is conceivable that the Action–Strategy Model could also be used to bring about change in these larger systems, however, as discussed in Chapter 8 of the text.

Point #4: Savvy Workers—Strong Clients/Consumers.   Direct service social workers are uniquely suited to initiate change in their agencies. As stated earlier, who knows better what needs to be done to improve the quality of service for clients/consumers? Direct service social workers interact with clients/consumers more frequently than middle management and higher administration personnel. Before front-line workers set out to change an agency policy, however, they must form professional relationships with staff in their agency to learn all of their functions and to assess the larger picture. Direct service workers should avoid pigeon-holing themselves into one small corner or service area of their organization. They must reach out and form coalitions with agency members as well as with staff in other community organizations.

Client vs. Consumer.   It is difficult to refrain from using the word "client" when describing persons who seek social work services. Even though the term "client" connotes powerlessness and weaknesses in a person—one who is in need of treatment or fixing—it continues to be widely used in social work literature despite efforts on the part of some authors and practitioners to the contrary (DuBois & Miley, 1992). The term *"client"* carries with it the idea that the person who is asking for help is powerless and that the worker possesses the knowledge, ability, and authority to control the situation, albeit for success. This type of thinking flies in the face of the helping process dubbed as a "joint decision making process" that is supposed to occur between the workers and persons seeking help. The word *"consumer"* may be more appropriate as a consumer has the ability to decide the who, what, where, when, how, and why of requesting help to meet a need and what agency can best assist with that process. Consumers are also represented in all systems levels in the hierarchal structure of social systems discussed in Chapter 2. Persons who are involuntarily mandated to human service agencies also retain the ability to choose services provided within the specified organization or setting and can still exercise choice, although their options are most likely reduced given the circumstances of the mandate such as a court order, jail sentence, or incarceration in a prison.

The underlying value and one that girds the profession of social work when employing the terms "clients and consumers" is that of self-determination. It is not the goal of social work practice to make those seeking help dependent on workers and agencies, but rather to empower them so that they become capable of deciding and choosing the course of action that best meets their needs. While we prefer the use of the word "consumer" to describe those persons who seek assistance from professional social workers, we have chosen the phrase *clients/consumers* when speaking of those who request assistance or are required to seek treatment in human service agencies. It seems that the terms "client" and "consumer" are used interchangeably in many texts. The word "client" almost seems to have taken on a new life and meaning of its own in today's social work circles of practice, research, and scholarship—one that is, perhaps, different from ideas about how the word was used during the first several decades of the twentieth century.

Even more important, when thinking about clients/consumers, is that the strengths of those persons who seek help must be respected. The Action–Strategy Model is based on the belief that clients/consumers of an organization possess strengths that can be tapped by the professional change agent throughout the agency policy change process. The social worker must bring clients/consumers along with them in the process whenever possible. All too often, they are overlooked and their views and ideas are ignored by professional social workers. Tapping into the social, psychological, and physical strengths of clients/consumers and deciding a plan of action and a change strategy that builds on strengths rather than weaknesses, complements the idea of "empowerment" in social work practice.

Empowerment.   The term "empowerment" is widely used in the social work literature. *Empowerment* in social work practice is defined in *The Social Work Dictionary* as "the process of helping individuals, families, groups, and communities increase their personal, interpersonal, socioeconomic and political strength and develop influence toward improving their circumstances" (Barker, 1999). The idea of empowerment in social work can be traced to the early beginnings of the profession during the latter part of the nineteenth century in America (Simon, 1994). In her book, *The Empowerment Tradition in American Social Work*, Simon discusses the major contributions of many social work authors who have written about empowerment including Pinderhughes, Solomon, Germain and Gitterman, Ross, Guitterez, Falck, and Grosser. Simon summarizes her discussion about empowerment practice from 1945–1994, as follows:

> empowering aspects of social work practice since 1945 include carefully sequenced interventions that respond first to needs and issues clients have highlighted as primary, active encouragement of clients' participation in mutual aid networks, and the fullest possible involvement of formerly disenfranchised clients—in collaboration with a responsive and accountable professional and governmental corps—in contouring the programs that serve them and the environs in which they live their lives (Simon, 1994).

Drawing from these ideas, *empowerment in agency policy change* in this text refers to the feelings and thinking about oneself that are based on personal competence, confidence, and objectivity necessary to engage in a change process that may result in an improved agency policy to better serve clients/consumers. The feelings and thoughts are found in both the professional social worker and whomever else is brought along in the process including clients/consumers. Whenever and wherever possible, social workers engaged in agency policy change must identify roles for clients/consumers. This approach does not mean, however, that the change effort is invalid if clients/consumers are not involved. Workers are indirectly involving clients/consumers when they reflect in their actions what their clients/consumers have told them regarding their needs, or if a policy is unjust and undemocratic. If clients/consumers are indirectly involved in a specific agency policy change, this does not diminish attempts to encourage them to sit on advisory boards or serve on organizational committees, for example. Agency policy change requires a certain amount of risk, especially for direct service workers. It means that savvy workers and strong clients/consumers participate, and commit to, whenever possible, the process throughout each stage of the Action–Strategy Model. When social workers and clients/consumers collaborate in this type of change effort, they re-emphasize a basic tenet of our profession and give new meaning to the age-old phrase: "Start where the client is!"

Point #5: Social Work Values and the Code of Ethics.   The core values of service, social justice, dignity and worth of the person, importance of human relationships, integrity, and competence (*NASW Code of Ethics*, August, 1996) always guide the social worker and allies through the proposed change process and through each stage and phase of the Model.

There are six components of Ethical Standards included in the *NASW Code of Ethics*. The final, or sixth, section guides social workers in their interventions of social welfare policy and provides the sanction and inspiration for social workers to engage in policy practice. The Standards are based on the professional values and ethical principles that are listed and explained in the beginning section of the Code. The standards for social welfare policy practice, Section 6, are as follows.

Section 6.   Social Workers' Ethical Responsibilities to the Broader Society

6.01   Social Welfare

Social workers should promote the general welfare of society, from local to global levels, and the development of people, their communities, and their environments. Social workers should advocate for living conditions conducive to the fulfillment of basic human needs and should promote social, economic, political, and cultural values and institutions that are compatible with the realization of social justice.

6.02   Public Participation

Social workers should facilitate informed participation by the public in shaping social policies and institutions.

6.03   Public Emergencies

Social workers should provide appropriate professional services in public emergencies to the greatest extent possible.

6.04   Social and Political Action

(a) Social workers should engage in social and political action that seeks to ensure that all people have equal access to the resources, employment, services, and opportunities they require to meet their basic human needs and to develop fully. Social workers should be aware of the impact of the political arena on practice and should advocate for changes in policy and legislation to improve social conditions in order to meet basic human needs and promote social justice.

(b) Social workers should act to expand choice and opportunity for all people, with special regard for vulnerable, disadvantaged, oppressed, and exploited people and groups.

(c) Social workers should promote conditions that encourage respect for cultural and social diversity within the United States and globally. Social workers should promote policies and practices that demonstrate respect for difference, support the expansion of cultural knowledge and resources, advocate for programs and institutions that demonstrate cultural competence, and promote policies that safeguard the rights of and confirm equity and social justice for all people.

(d) Social workers should act to prevent and eliminate domination of, exploitation of, and discrimination against any person, group, or class on the basis of race, ethnicity, national origin, color, sex, sexual orientation, age, marital status, political belief, religion, or mental or physical disability.

Point #6: A Systematic Process.   The Action–Strategy Model introduces a systematic process that can be used by social workers to change an agency policy in a community human service organization. It includes a dream component wherein the social worker wonders why a policy situation exists. Dreaming and wondering about the policy situation eventually conjures an idea about how the policy situation can potentially be changed or improved. In the analysis phase or Component II of the Model, systems theory is used to explain the policy situation in the context of the agency and community. A working hypotheses is formulated based on the information contained in the analysis. The hypothesis sets up the plan of action for the creation of the change goal/idea which is included in Component III of the Model. The plan of action takes into account the strengths of the *allies* (those who assist the social worker with the change), the target systems both *immediate* (those who will approve the agency policy change) and *ultimate* (those who will benefit from the agency policy change). The plan also sets the scene for the development of the strategy to be employed to link the allies' system to the larger target systems of the agency power structure and clients/consumers of services. As the allies concentrate on implementing the change strategy, they constantly elicit feedback from those involved in the process so that undesirable consequences will be reduced. The overall effort culminates in Component IV of the Model as the plan for goal fulfillment is realized based on a contract that is drafted between the allies and target systems. The focus of this agreement drives the plan of agency policy change into action. The Action–Strategy Model incorporates critical thinking and social systems theory.

The six star foundation points represent thoughts and ideas that encompass a mix of theoretical perspectives, practice wisdom and knowledge, ethical considerations and the value base of the profession. They provide social workers with the knowledge needed to help them gain information about the larger environment prior to the application of the Model. The final star point, "A Systematic Approach," leads the worker to Component I of the Action–Strategy Model. An overview is now presented.

An Overview.   There are four major components in the Action–Strategy Model. These are as follows:

    I. Dream about Agency Policy Change
    II. Analyze the Policy Situation Related to the Change Idea
    III. Develop a Plan of Action Related to Change Goal/Idea
    IV. Implement Change Strategy to Accomplish Approval of Agency Policy Change

Please note the use and placement of the words "dream, change idea, goal, and agency policy change." The change process progresses from a dream to reality as each component unfolds and is completed. The Action–Strategy Model provides a way to deal with this reality by tempering it with rationality, feasibility, and a commitment to values and ethics of the profession of social work.

Evolution of the Action–Strategy Model

Before we present an expanded outline of the Action–Strategy Model and a case example to illustrate a policy situation to which it could be applied to bring about agency policy change, information about the evolution of that particular Model is in order. Approximately two decades ago, the authors developed an undergraduate class in social welfare policy which was required for all social work majors. That class, which focused on social change theory, included a series of written assignments to demonstrate how change in agency policy could be accomplished. Drawing on the definition of "model" as stated by Kettner (1985) as a "coherent set of directives, . . . a pattern of symbols, rules, and processes, . . . (and) and statement of what the practitioner is expected to do," and as the need for updated theory more specifically relevant for the class arose, the authors began integrating newer theory and revising writing assignments. Eventually the Action–Strategy Model was developed because no existing models at the time sufficiently met classroom need. Written assignments had always required students to develop a plan of action for a policy change in their field placement agencies. These plans of action were for classroom purposes and were not required to be implemented. They did, however, require students to work closely with their agency field supervisors in completing the assignments. The authors discovered that many agencies, in fact, utilized the student work to successfully change agency policy. The model has been revised over the years to reflect the experience of students in their placement agencies.

An Outline of the Action–Strategy Model[1]

I. **DREAM ABOUT AGENCY POLICY CHANGE**
   A. Dream Away About a Better Way of Service for Clients/Consumers *in Your Agency*
   B. Tell Your Co-Workers About Your Dream
   C. Trust Yourself and Your Feelings
   D. Believe That It Is Possible to Live Your Dream

II. **ANALYZE THE POLICY SITUATION RELATED TO THE CHANGE IDEA**
   A. Formulation of the Question About the Agency Policy Change and Identification of the Policy Situation
      1. An existing written policy needs changing
      2. An unwritten policy needs formalizing
      3. No policy exists; one needs to be developed
   B. Determine the Location of the Agency Policy
      1. A policy within an agency
      2. A policy outside an agency
   C. Determine the Change Idea
   D. Analyze the Structure of the Agency and Community Related to the Change Idea

[1]Copyright © 1997, Ann Rae and Wanda Nicholas-Wolosuk, presented at the Annual Conference of the National Association of Social Workers, Michigan Chapter, on May 7, 1997.

  E. Assess Possible Undesirable Consequences of Change Including Resistance

  F. Formulate a Working Hypothesis About the Policy Situation

III. DEVELOP A PLAN OF ACTION RELATED TO THE CHANGE GOAL/IDEA

  A. Identify and Mobilize the Allies

    1. Rally the allies within and/or outside the agency

    2. Assess the strengths of the allies

  B. Determine the Needs of the Policy Situation

  C. Identify the Target Systems

    1. The immediate target system

    2. The ultimate target system

    3. Identify and assess the strengths of immediate and ultimate target systems

  D. Select an Appropriate Change Strategy

    1. Cooperation and collaboration

    2. Campaign

    3. Contest

      a. Contention

      b. Conflict

  E. Develop a Preliminary Contract for Implementation of Agency Policy Change

    1. Identify and state the goal (goal setting)

    2. Identify and state the objectives (objective setting)

    3. Tie the objectives to measurement and outcomes

  F. Develop a Plan for Evaluation of Agency Policy Change

    1. Evaluation of plan is ongoing throughout the implementation of the change process

    2. Final measurement follows implementation of the change process

  G. Develop a Plan for Stabilization of Agency Policy Change

  H. Develop a Plan for Eliminating or Decreasing Effects of Undesirable Consequences and Resistance

IV. IMPLEMENT CHANGE STRATEGY TO ACCOMPLISH APPROVAL OF AGENCY POLICY CHANGE

  A. Evaluate and Adjust for Resistance and Undesirable Consequences to Agency Policy Change

  B. Present Proposed Change to Decision Makers by:

    1. Use of position papers

    2. Making oral presentations

    3. Development of funding proposals

    4. Application of electronic technology such as creation of agency home pages, use of World Wide Web, statistical data analysis, and use of research methods for future decision-making

  C. If Approval Is Obtained, Develop a Final Contract for Implementation of Agency Policy Change

    1. Identify and state goal

    2. Identify and state objectives

    3. Tie objectives to measurement and outcomes

A case example is now presented to demonstrate how the four major components of the Action–Strategy Model provide a framework for agency staff to engage in a change process. In the example, staff activities commence with the dream stage and then move to the analysis phase. Their work continues with the formulation and development of the change idea/goal. As the case example unfolds, the final step of implementation of the plan to bring about the desired change completes the effort.

A Case Example of an Agency Policy Situation

I. DREAM ABOUT AGENCY POLICY CHANGE

A group of social workers had a dream of meeting the needs of a group of clients underserved in the community and at the same time continuing existing services to another group of vulnerable clients in spite of threatened budget cuts.

A Child and Family Service Agency is located in a county that is mid-size and composed of two urban centers surrounded by suburbs and several rural farming communities. Two years ago, a policy was developed and approved by the Agency Board, which resulted in a Home Help & Respite Care Program (HHRC). The HHRC Program is under contract to the State Department of Social Services. It currently services a caseload of 50 persons who are aged and 30 of whom are receiving home help, while the other 20 are receiving respite care. This is the newest program of the agency.

There is a seven-member Board of Directors. The chairperson of the Board is committed to maintaining cost-effectiveness in the budget as are most of the other members. All of the Board members, however, have an equally strong commitment to having the agency provide quality services to clients, and to maintaining the agency credibility in the community.

Agency funding is 60 percent United Way, 20 percent fees and 20 percent contracts. The State Department contract is 8 percent of the total budget. The HHRC policy that was adopted by the Board and developed into a program is very popular in the county and has been useful in fundraising by United Way.

The contract from the State Department is for $60,000, of which 15 percent is for administration and overhead. The rest is for service delivery and staff. The program staff is composed of five paraprofessionals and a half-time MSW supervisor. This person also recruits volunteers to assist the paraprofessionals. The Child and Family Service staff is composed of twenty professionals, all but four of whom are MSWs. The other four are two BSWs and two clinical psychologists. The professional staff has a median of five years experience. The director is an experienced social worker. This is her first administrative position, however. She has held the position for three years since arriving from another state. The director has been somewhat successful in local political contacts, but is still unfamiliar with state government. Her work background makes her very aware of the politics of local bureaucracies, but less aware of state-wide partisan politics.

She is wary of coming on too strong on this issue because she does not want to endanger other possible contracts from the State Department.

The State Department of Social Services informed the agency that it would not renew the contract as part of a necessary cutback in expenditures. The Child and Family Service agency director has recommended that the agency should eliminate the program, including releasing the paraprofessionals and the half-time MSW supervisor. This decision was made following discussion between only the director, assistant director, and program manager. The director is an authoritarian, aggressive administrator who in her three years at the agency has increased its size. She also was active in recruiting about half of the current Board. The Board typically supports her recommendations.

Staff learned of the Director's recommendation shortly after it was made. They were stunned and shocked to hear about the situation and immediately began to wonder if the HHRC program could be salvaged. Individually, they began to contemplate ways that they might be able to affect change and present alternatives with the hope of reversing the recommendation of the Director.

II. **ANALYZE THE POLICY SITUATION RELATED TO THE CHANGE IDEA**
Several services staff members met informally, because of their concern about the need for home help and respite services to the elderly population in their county. No other agency had any plan to provide such services. Among those staff were three who expressed their concern about another underserved population: the developmentally disabled. The group began to consider how to respond to the Director's recommendation. The staff members decided that a strategy must be adopted to find an alternative solution to the funding problem. They knew that a Board meeting would be held in approximately 30 days. The first step taken by the staff group was to gather, organize, analyze, and prepare all the available data on the HHRC program since its inception. They were careful to organize and prepare the data in several ways, such as narrative reports, posters, graphs, charts, transparencies. They paid particular attention to accuracy in gathering and interpreting the data. They contacted several consumers of services of the threatened program, who had recently responded to a customer satisfaction survey, and invited them to join their effort. Four persons showed up for their next meeting.

III. **DEVELOP A PLAN OF ACTION RELATED TO THE CHANGE GOAL/IDEA**
At that time, staff made a very bold decision to try to save the existing program not only by seeking alternative funding, but by asking the Board to change the existing policy to expand home help and respite care services to include developmentally disabled, as well as the aged. Their belief was that there was funding available for such services for the developmentally disabled. They agreed that attempting action at the state level, at this time, was beyond their ability in terms of time and effort that would be required.

Next, they requested a meeting between themselves, the consumer representatives, and the agency Director. They made the Director aware of their interest and their intention to try and save the program. While a little surprised that her recommendation was not automatically accepted by staff, the Director seemed impressed with the involvement of consumers, and albeit reluctantly, agreed to let them "try to save it, if they could, without alienating the Department." She did not offer to assist them, other than to allow them access to necessary information, and approve a small number of hours a week to work on this.

Through subsequent meetings, they then developed an action plan which was focused on two targets of their persuasive efforts. One target was the Board of Directors of the agency. The other target was the local United Way. The focus on the local United Way was led by an agency supervisor who had been with the agency for eight years. She had worked with many community organizations and was, at that time, a member of the local United Community Services Committee and the local Association of Retarded Citizens (ARC).

With the assistance of a committee of four staff and two consumers of service, they began to make contact with community agencies. The leader of this committee made contacts with those community organizations with which she was currently involved, and shared names of key contact persons in other organizations with group members so that all would have speedy access to relevant persons and organizations. They also began circulating information and inviting input from agency staff in other programs. Each agency director contacted was provided with information and letters of support were solicited in preparation for a desired meeting with United Way. Throughout all contacts, emphasis was placed on the fact that United Way viewed the program favorably and that its proven usefulness in fundraising made it valuable to other programs within the community. The committee leader agreed to take responsibility for arranging a meeting with key people at United Way, for the purpose of exploring the possibility of funding for the portion of the program that served the elderly population. The results of this meeting were tentatively positive, and information was prepared to be shared at the next Board of Directors meeting of their agency.

Meanwhile, another small group of staff and consumers, led by an agency supervisor (MSW) with ten years experience in the agency and who was currently a member of the local ARC, was also active. They focused their attention on securing permission from the Board of Directors to submit a proposal for a contract with the local Community Mental Health office to provide respite care to developmentally disabled persons. To submit such a proposal would require that the Board amend the policy that originally initiated the HHRC program, so that such services could be provided. They approached Directors who had been on the Board for several years, or had been recruited by the agency Director, but were known to be particularly supportive of the HHRC program. In those contacts they solicited support and asked for assistance in saving the program. They submitted a formal request for inclusion on the agenda at the next Board meeting.

IV.   **IMPLEMENT CHANGE STRATEGY TO ACCOMPLISH APPROVAL OF AGENCY POLICY CHANGE**

In preparation for this meeting, staff involved in the change effort gathered data from several agencies that provided other types of services to developmentally disabled citizens and their families. They developed a form with which they could survey the need for respite care services, and used it in each agency interview. They were also able to obtain agreement from three agencies to send the survey form to their clients. From this they were able to receive input from twenty different families, and together with information from the agency's staff, they were able to preliminarily assess the need for respite care services. They also interviewed the local Community Mental Health Director, based on their knowledge of his outspoken support of expansion of services that would support families of clients in their system. His philosophy was that providing services to clients was not sufficient; that the most effective services to clients of his agency involved families of those clients as well. They were able to convince him that the respite care services they would propose, contingent on their Board approval, would be supportive of families and clients. He indicated a willingness to support such a proposal and to present it to the local County Commissioners. He also agreed to put this philosophy and his commitment in writing to their agency Board.

Both groups met together to compare progress throughout the effort; and, both groups met jointly with the agency director to ensure that she was aware of their actions, and that she was willing for them to share their information with the Child and Family Service Board. By the time of the next Board of Directors meeting, both groups had completed all the contacts and interviews, had several letters of support, and had organized a comprehensive presentation that included use of audio/visual materials and equipment. In this presentation they emphasized the following points: the existing program was highly favored in the community; gave the agency high credibility; and was useful to United Way in fundraising; the services they provided to elderly clients were cost effective as compared to the cost of out-of-home care, which would be necessary for many of their clients should the services not be available; the addition of respite care to developmentally disabled would bring a new client group into the agency and was a service desired in the community. They presented their recommendation to apply for funding from United Way in order to continue the home help and respite care for elderly, and presented a draft of a suggested funding proposal. Then they recommended to the Board that the existing policy be revised to include respite care for developmentally disabled and provided written copies of the new recommended policy. Finally, they requested that the Board approve submission of a contract proposal to Community Mental Health and provided copies of the letter from the Community Mental Health and a draft of a suggested contract proposal. Obviously surprised by the comprehensiveness of their presentation and the supporting data, the agency director spoke up and added her support to all three proposals. After much discussion, the Board approved the solicitation of funding from United Way and from Community Mental Health. They approved the development of a revision to the existing policy, to become effective only upon approval of a Community Mental Health contract. They instructed the director to develop a contract, with the help of the staff involved in the change effort, which would be a plan of action for implementation of the approved changes. Agency staff saw this success as a beginning of a new working relationship with the agency director, and felt they had been able to impact a system, both within their agency and within the community, to the benefit of the client population.

Discussion of the Case Example

As is illustrated in the preceding case example, the four components of the Action–Strategy Model can guide social workers and their allies in the agency policy change process. The overall goal of the staff at the Child and Family Service Agency was to develop a plan of action to convince a decision-making body that an agency policy about respite care for the elderly needed to be re-examined and expanded to serve the developmentally disabled population as well. The social workers and their *allies*—those who dreamed about and designed the change process—and the clients/consumers of the proposed change came together to make their dream a reality. They worked together in a joint decision-making process and brought about change from within as well as outside of their agency system. Their dream became an idea about how an agency policy could be changed. It proceeded to an analysis of the policy situation, a change strategy selection, a plan of action, and goal development. It ended with a proposal presentation of key staff for the local United Way Planning Board of Directors.

As presented in the Preface, the Action–Strategy Model is focused on a step-by-step plan for accomplishing agency policy change. It is not intended to be a model for analyzing or for implementing policy. It is our belief that the tasks involved in the various components of the change process addressed by the Model are the ones for which policy practitioners are least prepared regardless of whether they are direct service workers, middle management staff, or executive administrators.

The other necessary tasks in policy practice, such as analysis and evaluation of public policy, are addressed in other ways in social work curricula. These models are presented in texts such as *American Social Welfare Policy: A Pluralist Approach* (2002) by Karger and Stoesz, *Integrating Social Welfare Policy and Social Work Practice* (1994) by McInnis-Dittrich, and *Social Welfare: Politics and Public Policy* (2000) by DiNitto. Implementation of policy is also addressed in those works. The topic of policy evaluation, in addition to being included in the instruction in social welfare policy courses, is also addressed in research methods classes, using such texts as *Evaluation: A Systematic Approach* (1999) by Rossi, Freeman, and Lipsey (1999), *Social Work Research and Evaluation Skills* (1998) by Frederic G. Reamer, and *Evaluating Practice: Guidelines for the Accountable Professional* (1999) by Bloom, Fischer, and Orme.

Summary

The Action–Strategy Model invites social workers to apply an intervention approach tailored to fill gaps in service delivery and prevent clients/consumers from further falls. The Action–Strategy Model rests on six star foundation points that are its foundation. These points include an incremental or "muddling through" process to affect change; a bottom-up approach; the belief that macro social work practitioners are direct service workers; the power of savvy workers, strong clients/consumers; the permeation of social work values and the Code of Ethics; and a systematic process throughout all steps of the Model.

Most social workers are warm, caring, and loving professionals who are also analytical thinkers. They want to "help people" but realize that their helping must be executed in an effective and efficient manner. What better way to begin than to open the window of opportunity caused by the massive shifts in funding and program development at the federal and state levels that continue to ripple and devolve throughout the social welfare system and to initiate new and creative policies at the local level?

The processes and steps in the Action–Strategy Model lead the social worker from dreams to questions, to ideas, to explanations, to strategy selection, to goal setting, and finally to planning for goal fulfillment and change to benefit clients and consumers of human services. Each phase and step of the Action–Strategy Model serves as a guide to bringing about change in agency policy that can result in "helping people." Content in Chapters 4, 5, and 6 contains an in-depth discussion of the major components of the Model. Throughout these chapters, events in the case example are linked to the stages and steps associated with each of the major components.

Important Terms and Phrases

Allies	Muddling through
Bottom-up approach to change	Social work macro practice
Clients/consumers	Solution-based incrementalism
Empowerment	Target systems
Empowerment in agency policy change	immediate
Incrementalism	ultimate

*Learning Exercises*_____

Review the case example in this chapter. Then answer the following questions as though you were a social worker in the agency and you desired continuation of the home help and respite program.

1. If there was no influential professional in the community who was already interested in respite services for developmentally disabled, would you have proposed saving *and expanding* existing respite services?

2. What would you have done if your agency director had objected to efforts to save the program? What issues would you consider in deciding whether to proceed?

3. Identify other possible plans to save the agency home help and respite care services. Then identify the steps you would take in at least one of them.

Study Questions _____

1. In what way does solution-based incrementalism differ from incrementalism?

2. Should agency policy change be initiated only from the top down? Why? Why not?

3. Direct service workers often do not envision themselves as macro workers. Explain why they should.

4. Based on your observations of the operations of a human service agency with which you are familiar, how are clients/consumers of services viewed by professional social workers?

5. Do you think that social workers in the human service agency feel comfortable about involving clients/consumers in an agency policy change? Do you think that professional social workers view clients/consumers from a "strengths perspective" (clients have strengths that can help to meet their needs) or from a "problem perspective" (clients are dependent and weak)?

6. What are your views regarding the "strengths perspective" and the "problem perspective"?

7. Explain how Section 6 of the Social Work Code of Ethics relates to social workers and agency policy change.

Explanation and Application
of the Model

Components I and II

Goal Statement _____

To demonstrate how the first two components of the Action–Strategy Model, Dream About Agency Policy Change and Analyze the Policy Situation Related to the Change Idea, can be used by social workers as they initially dream, analyze and hypothesize about a change idea that is beneficial to clients/consumers.

Discussion

The six star points that form the foundation of the Model and its four components were introduced and discussed in Chapter 3. Now, Components I and II of the Model, which contain guidelines for analysis of the policy situation, are presented.

The Model relies on *prescriptive knowledge* because a series of solution-based incremental steps are set forth to be worked through by the social worker and allies. "*Prescriptive knowledge* is knowledge about how to intervene, to act so that what can be predicted to occur can be changed or avoided" (Weinbach, 1998). In the way of review, the four major components of the Action–Strategy Model are shown in Figure 4.1.

Let us now proceed to a detailed discussion of how the major processes and specific steps in the Model can be applied from beginning to end.

The Action–Strategy Model

FIGURE 4.1

Component I—Dream About Agency Policy Change

Imagine you are a volunteer, field placement student, or social worker in an adult protective services unit of a public welfare organization where investigations are undertaken about mentally disabled and elderly persons who are suspected of being physically, psychologically, or sexually abused. Or, perhaps you work as a treatment specialist who conducts group work for delinquent youth in a residential treatment facility, or as a family therapist who specializes in marital counseling in an outpatient mental health setting.

Retreat from reality for a while and conjure up a few ideas about how you and other professional staff in your agency could serve clients/consumers in a more humane, creative, and effective manner. Next, contemplate these questions:

Have you always dreamed about creating something "special" that would give you the opportunity to "help people" in the most fulfilling and satisfying way?

Have you always dreamed about working with a network of other professionals and enjoying their emotional and intellectual support as you seek to achieve a desired goal?

Have you always dreamed about validating yourself as a professional, acting on your dreams and accomplishing a goal?

If the answers to the above questions are "yes," then dream on, but begin to temper your dreams with reality. There will be times in your professional life when you will want to act on your dreams to make them come true and take form. Do not be constrained by doubts about your competence and self-worth. After all, you will be equipped with the education, knowledge, practice skills, and ethical standards that prepare you to function as a professional social worker. Trust yourself and your ideas and share them with respected colleagues in your agency. Consider all of the possible ways that you could create an environment in your agency that would improve service delivery. Prioritize two or three of your ideas that are most important that will benefit clients/consumers. Remember that direct service social workers are well aware of the policies, programs, and services in their agencies that help or hurt their clients/consumers. Eventually your dream will take shape and proceed through the steps depicted in the flow chart (Figure 4.2).

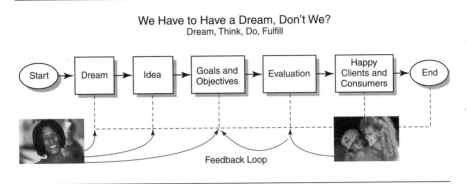

We Have to Have a Dream, Don't We?
Dream, Think, Do, Fulfill

FIGURE 4.2

As the change process evolves, the thoughtful social worker, however, recognizes both positive and negative feelings when contemplating acting on the dream and the idea of changing an agency policy. The knowledgeable social worker relies on intellect and rationality after weighing the negative and positive aspects of the feelings about change. The skillful social worker realizes that there may be risks attached to the idea of bringing about an agency policy change. The effective social worker realizes that thoughts and actions are extensions of feelings and emotions, and that the winning combination of "soft-hearted and hard-headed" characteristics (Gibbs, 1991) is unbeatable when it comes to making decisions about the future direction of an agency policy change.

Model Application to Case Example

In the case example presented in Chapter 3, the director of the agency has made a decision to recommend to the Board of Directors elimination of a program and release of professional and para-professional staff from the organization. The policy situation involving those staff who are desirous of salvaging the program is replete with political and economic considerations. The staff, however, have relied on the home help program for their elderly clients. They have even recognized, based on questions and comments from families and workers in other community agencies, that there is a need to expand the program to include services for disabled clients/consumers. Staff members come together to discuss the policy situation based on these considerations and begin to brainstorm as to how they can intervene to benefit the clients/consumers of the agency. As the workers coalesce around the policy situation they are imagining outcomes that might be forthcoming. They trust one another enough to share their feelings about the demise of the program and believe that it may be possible to change an existing policy situation. The activities of coming together and attempting to generate solutions on the part of staff in the case example integrate with Component I of the Action–Strategy Model, Dream About Agency Policy Change.

Component II—Analyze the Policy Situation Related to the Change Idea

Now let us turn the discussion to the second major component in the Model that is concerned with the analysis of a policy situation currently of interest in an agency. A *policy situation* is defined as the manner in which policy, or the lack thereof, is currently impacting client/consumer well being. The policy may be an agency policy, an intra-agency policy, or a policy from outside the agency that must be implemented by the agency. Before presenting the aspects of this process in greater detail, it is important to think about agency policy situations that give rise to initiating change. When examining the following examples of policy situations, be mindful that procedures and forms **flow from** policy, but essentially, cannot be thought of as policies. Here are some policy situations that may require development or improvement.

Emergency Medical Care procedures (when to resuscitate, for example) in an adult day care program

Proof of income verification forms for clients in a nongovernmental family and service agency

Referral procedures from community agencies for low-income children in an Early Head Start Program

Family planning services and confidentiality arrangements for teenage girls in a county public health department

Transportation by staff of wards of the court or children in foster care placement and residential treatment facilities in a juvenile court

Criminal background check policies for employees, applicants for employment, and volunteers in medical long-term care facilities

Guardianship procedures for the institutionalized mentally ill in a probate court division

Discipline policy for staff use in a Boys and Girls Club

Outreach programs for nursing home selection by family members in rural counties in an area agency on aging

Visitation privileges by nonfamily members in an inpatient residential substance abuse treatment center

Retention policy for failing students in elementary and middle public schools

Recruitment of volunteers for a Meals on Wheels Program in an aging agency

Staff education program for handling violent situations in a domestic violence shelter

Supervised home visits for at-risk families in a child abuse and neglect prevention program in a department of social services

Adoption policy for a single parent in a family and children's agency

Therapeutic touch and massage program procedures for nursing staff in an out-patient mental health clinic

Identification of child abuse injuries for child protective services referrals by school personnel in an elementary public school

Transportation vouchers for low-income working mothers in a rural public assistance agency

Release of information forms in a juvenile detention facility

Managed care procedures and privacy protection of clients in an out-patient mental health center

Information collected about the policy situation necessary to complete the second component of the Model comes from research about the agency and the community. Social work students often do not know where to begin the search to learn about human service agencies or community characteristics. Many students are fearful about interviewing the appropriate person to secure information. Where does one begin this type of research? Start with the phone book, for openers. It contains the names of all government agencies (local, state, regional, and federal), a section of businesses, and the Yellow Pages. United Way Planning Boards and voluntary action agencies publish directories on an annual basis that contain facts about the major human service organizations in local communities. The local library contains data about numerous local and state organizations that are public, nonprofit, and proprietary in nature. City and county planning units compile statistics about poverty levels, land use, and population projections. Staff in the local Chamber of Commerce are also available to answer questions and provide direction.

Also, do not overlook information that is furnished on the Internet and World Wide Web about local, state, and national organizations. Peruse the publication *The social worker's internet handbook*. This publication provides a wealth of practical information that is useful for social workers in any community agency (Grant & Grobman, 1998). Also of note is the recent publication, *Social Work and the Web*, which provides practical information about how social workers can make electronic technology work for them, including an introduction about how to construct an agency web page (Vernon & Lynch, 2000).

Social work students also learn that the skills with which they became familiar in basic interviewing courses are invaluable when embarking on a visit with a director of a human service organization, a program supervisor in an agency, or a community representative, for example. Have questions ready and then listen, listen, listen to the communication of the director or staff in these organizations in order to soak up the details and observe nuances of the conversation during the interview. Curiosity, preparation, the ability to listen, and a sense of enthusiasm are characteristics that will stand students and social workers in good stead as data is gathered for this component of the Model.

Here are specific suggestions and questions to guide your progress as you apply the Action–Strategy Model of Agency Policy Change in Component II of the Model, "Analyze the Policy Situation Related to the Change Idea."

Formulation of the Question About the Agency Policy Change and Identification of the Policy Situation

Does an Existing Written Policy Need Changing?

Does an Unwritten Policy Need Formalizing?

Does No Policy Exist and One Needs to Be Developed?

What is the existing policy situation that is causing tension, imbalance or stress in the agency system?

Is there an assumed pattern of behavior in operation on the part of the professional staff as they deliver services to clients/consumers, but no written policy about the delivery of such services?

Is there a complete lack of a policy regarding specific services for clients/consumers when it is obvious to professional staff that such services are needed?

Determine the Location of the Agency Policy

Is the Policy Situation Specific Solely to the Agency?

Is the Policy Situation Specific to a Part or Sub-part of the Community?

What is the general location of written agency policies?

Where are written policies found? For example, one might examine the agency manual for a policy regarding the responsibilities of juvenile probation officers. Or, ask to examine the Annual Report or minutes of the Agency Board of Directors. Perhaps, the policy situation that is producing tension in the agency is contained in an annual report to the stockholders if the organization is for-profit in nature.

What is the origin of the agency policy under analysis?

Is it the result of federal, state, local law, or formulated by a national governing board of directors? Or, is it strictly "local" in origin—indigenous to the professional staff of the agency or the Board of Directors? Why is this agency policy in operation in the agency? Who initiated or originated the policy? Did key members of the community help to create the agency policy, for example?

Determine the Change Idea

If there is an existing written policy, what is its purpose? If it is not written, what is its purpose? What is there about the policy situation—written, unwritten or non-existent that needs to be changed?

Who is the policy serving? What is the *target system*?

What are the general characteristics of the target system (those for whom the policy and service is intended) in this community: abused women, African-American minority elderly? For example, if the target system is the "aged living alone," how does the agency define "aged?"

What is the economic, political, and social status of the population in the community that the policy serves?

Can you think of a change idea regarding the policy situation that originated in your dream about how service delivery could be improved to benefit client/consumers in the agency?

Are you willing to share your ideas about the policy situation with clients/consumers to elicit their views?

Are you willing to share your ideas with other professional staff in your agency to elicit their views and thoughts about your change idea?

At this point in the process, can you specifically verbalize your change idea about the policy situation?

Write it down or type it on a word processor.

Analyze the Structure of the Agency and Community Related to the Change Idea

Examine the agency—its service delivery system and structure.

What are the characteristics of the service delivery system?

Does the agency exist or was it created to serve a special population group such as unemployed welfare recipients or the chronically mentally ill?

Does the agency exist or was it created to meet a special need in the community such as providing assistance for law enforcement and courts to help children who have allegedly been abused give testimony?

What is the agency sanction, legitimacy? Does it exist because of legislation? Does it exist because of community needs?

What is the purpose or mission of the agency and what needs does it meet for the population it serves?

What are the goals of the agency? Official goals? Unofficial goals?

What are the major programs and services of the agency? Are these congruent with the goals of the agency?

What is the cost of service delivery? Who has responsibility for budget preparation? What entity or group makes the final decisions involving the annual budget and financial arrangements?

How is the agency evaluated and regulated? Community standards? Board of Directors? Legislative mandate? Stockholders? Clients and Consumers?

Next, examine the agency structure.

Is there an organizational chart?

If one does not exist, can one be constructed to portray the formal system of the agency?

What is the organizational form of the agency? Is there an organizational theory that guides the agency—bureaucratic, open-systems, contingency, for example?

What are the administrative arrangements in the agency?

What are the professional staff arrangements in the agency?

What are the technological and clerical supports in the agency?

Is there a Board of Directors, an Advisory Commission, a volunteer component, a managed-care approval and credentialing system?

Based on your observations and interviews, can another chart be constructed that represents the informal system?

Who talks to whom? From whom does one seek help with specific kinds of problems? Who really gets things done?

Compare the charts of the formal and informal systems for similarities and differences between the two.

Examine the community—the home of the agency and its social systems and structure.

What are the social systems in operation in the community?

What is the history of the community?

What are its geographic boundaries?

What is the population? Has it decreased or increased during the past ten years? What are the projections?

What are the income levels?

What are the occupational levels?

What is the number of persons receiving public assistance, including children?

What is the make-up of race, religion, sex, age, ethnicity, cultures, and sub-cultures?

What is the family composition?

What is the unemployment rate?

What are the crime statistics?

What about health data—sexually transmitted diseases, HIV, AIDS, TB, infant mortality? Energy and waste management? Recycling and food use?

What are the major institutions in the community?

> For example, religious, schools, community colleges, universities; industries; social agencies such as youth and aging, domestic violence, food pantries; United Way Board; government agencies; political parties; newspapers; and cultural organizations?

The community structure.

> Based on your findings about the social systems in operation in the community, answer the following questions about the community structure:

> What are some significant types of groupings or social categories in the community—religious, political, nationality, racial, economic, cultural, social class, for example?

> What key institutions in the community have the greatest power, influence, or social utility?

> What is the position of human service agencies and personnel in this community?

> Is there an operating power structure in the community; what groups or individuals comprise it?

> What kind of leadership exists in the community?

> What forces in the community make for collaboration, conflict or insulation among groups?

> What are some outstanding or characteristic values that are typical of this community?

> What are the major social problems or issues in the community? Which groups seem to be central to resolving each issue; to intensifying it?

> What are the forces for change, resistant forces, and interference forces in operation in the community?

Links between the **agency** and **community** organizations.

> Examine the links between the agency and community organizations.

> Is there a duplication of services in the community? For example, if one is examining the current policy of the local aging agency about in-home services for the elderly, how would the delivery of these types of services correlate to in-home services provided by the Visiting Nurses Association?

> How well do human service agencies collaborate to reduce duplication and fragmentation of service delivery in the community?[1]

---

[1]The source of many of the questions about the community are contained in an information sheet that came into the possession of the authors several years ago. Unfortunately, there is no title, date, or author listed on the information sheet.

Assess Possible Undesirable Consequences
of Change Including Resistance

The desirable consequence of the change idea is to produce benefits that bring about an improved quality of life for clients/consumers of agency services. Harmful results are to be avoided at any cost. The worker must analyze and assess the change possibility thoroughly to avoid undesirable consequences. The idea of solution-based incrementalism can guide the social worker as this part of the Model unfolds.

Determination of the change idea is also compared to the rules of probability or the likelihood that the change idea will succeed. Will there be a ninety percent success rate? Seventy–five percent? The social worker realizes that it is easier to bring about change in smaller systems; the smaller the social system that is the target of change, the closer to it is the individual seeking the change. Also, the more modest the change, the more likely it is that the change will occur. Finally, the social worker realizes that the less ambitious the change, the easier it will be to achieve, and as support is sought for the change idea, he/she will begin to lose some degree of control over the change process. The social worker also realizes that there are, after all, numerous value problems associated with the "right to intervene," and many failures and harmful consequences may occur as a result of the change.

Here are specific questions that guide the worker in this section of Component II of the Model.

> What is the attitude about the policy situation that exists among workers, staff and the client/consumer system; and between the administration and the staff?

> Between the administration and the client/consumer system? Between the agency and the community? Between the target systems and the community?

> If possible, try to ascertain if the target system has the motivation, capacity and opportunity to engage in change efforts regarding the agency policy situation.

> What are the implicit and explicit cultural and social values served by the policy situation? Does it exist to maintain, control, or enhance the well-being of clients/consumers? For example, does an employment and training program exist mainly to provide marginally employable clients/consumers with something to keep them off the streets, or is the aim of the program to, indeed, prepare them for gainful employment?

> What are the predominant values that affect the client/consumers of the agency within the community? Is there a difference between the values of the agency clients/consumers and those in the larger community? What are these differences?

> Does this policy situation oppress or enhance the well-being of the clients/consumers? Does it discriminate against the clients/consumers? If so, how is this oppression and discrimination viewed by professional staff in the agency, other human service organizations and members of the larger community?

> If there is an existing agency policy situation that is causing imbalance in the agency system, how is it implemented or executed? Is there a difference in im-

plementation about what is actually stated and required and what is actually carried out inherent in the policy situation? If so, what and why?

Identify and list organizational and community barriers or resistance of elements to your change idea that have become obvious to you throughout the analysis of the policy situation.

At this time in the development of the Action–Strategy Model, it is likely that some form of resistance will occur. We now turn our discussion to the idea of resistance and the barriers that can emerge in the change process.

Resistance to the Idea of Change in General—The Six Deadly Barriers to Change.
Resistance to change is grounded in ignorance and in fear of the unknown. Change has to be seen as an opportunity by people—and then there will be no fear.—Peter F. Drucker

Social workers are familiar with the concept of resistance in the development of the therapeutic relationship. Resistance is the arousal of a psychological force that swells up against another force. Freud used the term to "identify a phenomenon which, from his viewpoint, had the effect of blocking the attainment of his therapeutic objectives." Resistance was viewed as a "necessary and even desirable aspect of the therapy" (Resnick & Patti, 1980). Resistance to change in many types of workplace situations ranging from industrial and manufacturing organizations to human service agencies has been discussed and analyzed during the last several decades of the twentieth century (Lewin, 1951; Katz & Kahn, 1966; Warren, 1977; Griffin & Moorhead, 1986; Kettner et al., 1985; Hall, 1991; Neugeboren, 1991; Hasenfeld, 1992; Huber, 1993; Huber & Glick, 1993; Gortner, Mahler, & Nicholson, 1997; Prasad & Prasad, 1998; Weinbach, 1998).

A definition of resistance offered by Rino J. Patti in 1974 appears to be as timely today regarding direct service workers who attempt to bring about change in a human service organization: "*Resistance* refers to those forces or conditions within the organization that tend to decrease the likelihood that decision makers will accept or act favorably upon a proposal for change initiated by an administrative subordinate" (Patti, 1974). Patti postulates that resistance presents itself in varying degrees as related to the nature of the "change proposal," or that part of a policy at which the change is aimed; the "value orientation of decision makers," or differences or similarities between the values about the direction of the agency held by administrators compared to the values about the direction of the agency held by direct service workers; the "organizational distance" or the number of administrative levels between the direct service workers and the administration with the success of the change proposal diminishing if the worker is several levels removed from the administration; and, the "sunk costs" or an "organizations' investment in some arrangement or pattern of behavior on the part of human and technological resources." It is useful for the social worker to identify resistance to change in agency policy situations because negative thoughts and ideas about change can easily be turned into positive statements and, eventually, into change goals.

Some easily understood possible sources of resistance to change identified by Warren (1977) are useful to keep in mind when assessing possible undesirable consequences of the change effort.

Habit—We do things in an accustomed way and it is difficult to change.

Disruption—We grow accustomed to the way things are and adjustment to change disturbs the status quo. Technological advances relate to this category.

Vested Interest—We benefit more from a situation when we have a "piece of the pie."

Ideology—We think that the change is in opposition to our deeply held beliefs and values.

Psychopathology—we view change similarly to the manner in which clients/consumers demonstrate an irrational reaction to counseling.

Rational Conviction—We find acceptable reasons for opposing change.

While these ideas were advanced several decades ago, they are germane to human service environments today. The ability to turn barriers to change caused by resistance into positive approaches can redirect the social worker and allies in the change effort. Resistance, however, is generally seen as an undesirable entity that must be overcome by the social worker and allies throughout the agency policy change process.

Formulate a Working Hypothesis About the Policy Situation

Summarize by stating a *working hypothesis* about *why* you think the policy situation exists and why the current agency policy or lack of one is producing tension and stress in the system. Your hypothesis is based on your analysis and answers to the preceding questions contained in Component II of the Action–Strategy Model and includes the following steps:

Identify what it is about the agency policy situation that you want to change.

Next, think about whom you would like to work with you as the process begins to further unfold.

Finally, ask the question: "Is it worth it?" If the answer is "yes," then proceed to Component III of the Action–Strategy Model of Agency Policy Change. If the answer is "no," then return to page 1 of this text and start to re-read the content. Pay particular attention to the questionnaire about the reasons that students pursue social work as a career and your answers to those questions. Next, re-examine Section 6 of the Code of Ethics in Chapter 3, the "Social worker's ethical responsibility to the broader society." Think about how you will act on the principles contained in this section when you begin your career as a professional social worker at either the BSW or MSW levels.

Model Application to Case Example

In the case example in Chapter 3, the direct service workers who wanted to save the home help program were attempting to answer the question: "Is it possible to maintain the existing program along with its staff and even expand it to serve the developmentally disabled?" The situation was that an existing policy was in jeopardy as the State Department of Social Services terminated a contract and eliminated funding for a Home Help & Respite Care Program administered by a community Child and Family Service agency. This written agency policy—the foundation of the home help respite for the elderly program and the program structure and development—was authorized by the Board of Directors and contained in the Board's monthly minutes. The program description, goals, and objectives that were developed from the policy were found in the agency manual. The professional staff in the family service agency set forth a change idea to not only continue the existing program but expand services to another population as well. Their actions were guided in a solution-based fashion. The workers examined the existing policy, the structure and integration of the program within their organization, the community, the budget and expenditures for service delivery, and the number of clients/consumers who had been serviced from its inception. The workers thought about barriers to change and the sources of resistance such as the director, Board of Directors, or other service workers in their agency who might think that saving the program would result in more work for them in their caseloads. The change idea of adopting a strategy to find an alternative solution to the funding problem within the next thirty days became the working hypothesis of the group and is associated with Component II of the Action–Strategy Model, Analyze the Policy Situation Related to the Change Idea.

The preceding questions and suggestions about Components I and II of the Model guide the social worker's analysis of the policy situation. It is crucial to address as many of these items as possible. The responses will assist the worker to make an informed decision regarding the all-important question of whether or not it is worthwhile to continue the change effort and proceed with the intervention. Also, during this time the social worker begins to identify staff, community representatives, and clients/consumers who are willing to help as the intervention unfolds. They will eventually become part of the allies as discussed in Component III of the Action–Strategy Model. Also, in Component III of the Model, "Develop a Plan of Action Related to the Change Goal/Idea," the phrase "change idea" is expanded to include the word "goal," to signify that the change idea is taking definite shape and the direction of the process, while still in the analysis and planning stages, is forward moving and outcome oriented.

Summary

When a social worker dreams about an agency policy change, he/she engages in thoughts about possible changes that would benefit clients/consumers. The dream phase of Component I is followed by the process of analysis in Component II that demands that the social worker and those who are supportive of the change get the facts and compare and contrast them to determine similarities and differences about the change idea. A thorough analysis assists the social worker in answering the questions: Is it worth it? How much do I value the intended change? Is it possible? Is it feasible? What will be the extent of the change? When the answers to these questions have been weighed, other questions emerge. How does the worker really know that a need exists? Who will help to implement the intended change and is it possible to enlist clients/consumers in the effort? What strategy approach will succeed? Finally, the essential question: Will our efforts result in an outcome that will benefit clients/consumers? Component II, Analyze the Policy Situation Related to the Change Idea, is critical for the social worker and allies to complete because it directs succeeding steps in the Action–Strategy Model in the next component, Develop a Plan of Action Related to the Change Goal/Idea. Content about this component is discussed next in Chapter 5.

Important Terms and Phrases

Prescriptive knowledge
Policy situation
Resistance
   habit
   disruption
   vested interest
   ideology
   psychopathology
   rational conviction

Target system
Working hypothesis

Learning Exercises

Identify a current issue in your local community that is directly impacting a social welfare policy in a human service agency with which you are familiar. Perhaps you have been a volunteer in this agency, or you are carrying out a field placement there. Perhaps there has been media coverage of an event regarding this agency in recent months and you have followed the story closely. Examples of such issues might include: lack of available jobs for single mothers required to work while receiving assistance or long waiting lists for treatment services for substance-abusing mothers. Now assume that you are part of a work group that has met to discuss this policy situation and plan a course of action.

1. How would you proceed if your group were asked by the middle management of the agency to briefly describe the policy situation and its location or specific service system within the agency? Where are the written policies found, for example? Would you ask to examine the annual report of the agency or a Board of Director's report regarding something relevant to the policy situation? What other methods, if any, can you think of for gathering information regarding the policy?

2. Next, assume your group has been asked to collect and assess relevant data for use as the members further identify and assess the policy situation. What would be your first step? How would you begin the collection and assessment process? Where would you look? Would you assess the community or a part of it that would be affected by the policy, for example? Would you begin your assessment in the organization? List and prioritize the appropriate steps that you think need to be undertaken.

3. Would your group invite clients/consumers of the agency who are affected by the policy situation to brainstorm the policy? If "yes," how would you involve clients/consumers? If "no," why not?

4. Decide which components of the identification and assessment process in Part II of the Action–Strategy Model would be critical to the formulation of a hypothesis about why the policy situation exists. Attempt to state such a hypothesis, regarding the identified policy, in no more than two paragraphs.

Study Questions _____

1. In applying the Action–Strategy Model of Agency Policy Change, what are some of the outcomes related to completion of Parts I and II?

2. A change in an agency policy often begins with someone having a "dream" about services to clients/consumers being better. How does one get from the initial dream to the formulation of an idea?

3. How do you define a policy situation?

4. Chapter 4 gives some examples of policy situations. Think of some additional examples from your own experience/knowledge.

5. What are some of the sources for information about human service agencies and the community?

6. Identify the necessary questions to ask in determining the change idea.

7. When initiating change, why does the social worker need to assess likely undesirable consequence?

8. Based on your observations of the operations of a human service agency with which you are familiar, have you witnessed any of the "six deadly barriers to change," discussed in this chapter? What do you think would be the most difficult barrier to overcome? What do you think would be the easiest barrier to eliminate when attempting policy change?

5

Explanation and Application of the Model

Component III

Goal Statement _____

To demonstrate how the third component of the Action–Strategy Model, Develop a Plan of Action Related to the Change Goal/Idea, can be used by social workers as they formulate a goal and move forward with the agency policy change process.

Discussion

The term *plan* is defined as the cognitive arrangement of activities in which the social worker and allies work together using an agreed-upon strategy to develop, implement, evaluate, and achieve an agency policy change that will benefit clients/consumers. The major focus of the Action–Strategy Model is the development of a plan and strategy about how to implement and evaluate an agency policy change. Part of the development of the plan is dependent on the identification, assessment, and mobilization of the allies, however. We now turn our thoughts to a few ideas about this group and why it is vital to the change effort.

Social Workers, Their Allies, and Policy Practice

The term *allies* is defined as those persons connected either by their likenesses or friendship, and by their values or interests or both, who unite to develop, implement, evaluate, and achieve an agency policy change that will benefit clients/consumers. The allies are those persons who persuade and induce the immediate (decision makers) and ultimate (clients/consumers) target systems to agree to the agency policy change. The motivation, capacity, and opportunity of these allies must constantly be bolstered and supported by the social worker who initially identifies the policy situation as an area of change. Social work values and ethics play a large role in guiding the social worker's behavior and relationships with the allies throughout all stages and phases of the agency policy change endeavor. The social worker who initially draws attention to the policy situation usually attempts to bring those persons with similar values into the alliance, but the make-up of this group also depends largely on the nature of the proposed change goal/idea.

Building on the information gained in the preceding analytical component of the Model, especially the activities undertaken to assess undesirable consequences of change including resistance, it is helpful to recall some insightful concepts set forth by Kurt Lewin (1951), who emphasized the significance of group participation and dynamics in bringing about change in social systems. Despite the fact that Lewin developed his ideas about social change several decades ago, his work remains meaningful today. Karl Weick and Robert Quinn (1999) in their article, "Organizational change and development," quote from the writing of Hendry as follows:

> Scratch any account of creating and managing change and the idea that change is a three-stage process which necessarily begins with a process of unfreezing will not be far below the surface. Indeed it has been said that the whole theory of change is reducible to this one idea of Kurt Lewin's.

Lewin stated that a "planned social change may be thought of as composed of unfreezing, change of level, and freezing on the new level. In all three respects group decision has the general advantage of the group procedure" (Lewin, 1951). He developed a method to engage in this process known as "field theory" from which the term "force field analysis" evolved. According to this theory, there is a force field surrounding every patterned behavior, which reflects the dynamics of human behavior occuring in constantly changing situations (Warren, 1977). Forces are constantly working to maintain a behavior pattern while other forces are constantly working to change it. Those forces that are operating for change or the "driving" forces must overcome or overpower the "restraining" forces if change is to occur (Lewin, 1951). Brager and Holloway (1978) in their text, *Changing Human Service Organizations*, relate that Lewin called the systematic identification of opposing forces, a "force field analysis." They state that force field analysis is important when the "worker has defined a change goal," and when identifying those colleagues whose support is needed to accomplish the desired change. These activities are similar to activities set forth in the initial part of the Action–Strategy Model: formulation of a working hypothesis about the policy situation in Component I, "F"; and, the identification and mobilization of the allies and assessment of their strengths in Component III, "A."

Once the social worker (change agent) has a clear understanding of the policy situation and has begun to think about what members of the organization might be brought along in the process, the next step is to list the "driving" and "restraining" forces that may appear in the change effort. These forces could also affect the composition of the allies and their motivation to engage in changing an agency policy. Brager and Holloway (1978) also add that if there is agreement among the allies that change is needed, the allies must subsequently concern themselves with whether or not the policy situation is "amenable to change." Further, the social worker and allies must examine the "forces potential for modification" and determine if they will be able "to alter it—to increase it if the force is a driving force, or to decrease it if it is a restraining force." Brager and Holloway continue their discussion of force field analysis with the thought that the forces must be analyzed for "potency" or the "impact it will have on effecting the goal" within the context of the driving (increasing the potential) or restraining (decreasing the potential) forces. Finally, their discussion turns to the introduction of the concept of "consistency" of the forces or the relative stability of the force as the social worker and allies move through the change process. These concepts are valuable as the worker initiates the steps contained in Component III of the Action–Strategy Model—Develop a Plan of Action Related to the Change Goal/Idea—and the composition of the allies. The choice of a strategy and development of the preliminary contract could also be influenced by the use of a force field analysis.

It is conceivable that administrators, direct service workers, and clients/consumers could work together regarding an agency policy change. The axiom of "politics makes strange bed fellows" may come into play as the allies often come together based on interest in the situation, and to a lesser extent on similarity in social background and education. An example of this would be the evolving concern about the power of managed care and health maintenance organizations and their impact on patient confidentiality. With over 90 percent of insured persons in managed care plans, professional staff and patients are interested in protecting the confidentiality of personal information, regardless of political ideology, economic status, or social and educational background.

It is also useful at this point to keep in mind some ideas presented in the text, *Taking Action in Organizations and Communities* (Erlich, Rothman, & Teresa, 1999), in which guidelines are set forth to encourage participation of interested persons in a change effort. The idea of benefits is discussed in their text as follows: "Practitioners wishing to foster participation in organizations, voluntary associations, or task groups should provide (or increase) appropriate benefits." The term "participation" in this guideline includes the "recruitment of new members, but also changes in the pattern of existing members' participation."

There must be some form of pay-off or reward that will accrue to a social worker and allies who engage in change—some type of *benefit*, that is. Benefits consist of "instrumental" and "expressive." *Instrumental* benefits result if the agency policy change will indeed result in some type of improved service for clients/consumers. *Expressive* benefits are "intangible and psychological in character, such as increased friendships, personal satisfaction, and pride" (Erlich et al., 1999). It is critical that those who join the allies experience reinforcement from both benefit forms as appreciation for their efforts will likely increase the level of motivation needed to accomplish the agency policy change. Social work salaries are traditionally low considering the difficult type of work social workers undertake with clients/consumers. Clients/consumers who join the change effort often lack financial and emotional resources. It becomes all the more important that the social worker who initiates the change effort be aware that the allies must not only share an interest in the policy situation, but that "the gains to be seen from participating must outweigh the losses" (Warren, 1977). In other words, when the social worker and allies withdraw from the change action once the agency policy change has been approved, it would be encouraging if some reward or benefit would have been bestowed on them for their efforts.

When social workers team up with others who hold similar values in a change effort, they need to view themselves, their clients and consumers from a "strengths perspective," a concept discussed by Saleebey (1997). Perception of a person's or group's resources, not the actual resources possessed, strongly influences how others will behave toward that person or group. Building on this idea is the thought that if the allies who are attempting to bring about the agency policy change are perceived as strong and united, they will be treated as such. Therefore, the allies must commence the change effort from the strongest position possible in order to develop, plan, implement, and stabilize the change goal/idea. Negotiation with a decision-making body that is based on the strengths of the worker and allies is always preferable to negotiation based on weaknesses.

Social workers who "practice policy"—whether at the national, state, or local agency level—are essentially trying to influence a group of people to behave in a certain way. Hopefully, those being influenced will agree with the proposed change and it will become easier to execute. The fun starts when the group whom the social worker and the allies want to influence does not agree with the change and the social worker and allies attempt to win over the opposition.

Social workers, however, are somewhat uncomfortable with the idea of exerting influence and control over someone else as discussed in Chapter 2. The social worker attempting to bring about agency policy change recognizes that the control and cooperation of persons in the change process is not totally dependent on his or her ideas. The social worker keeps this idea in the back of his/her mind as the change process unfolds. His or her control will expand and decline and tradeoffs will occur throughout the change effort.

The social worker must also keep in mind just how much of the change idea can be compromised. It is always helpful to remind oneself that the "practice of policy" involves the art of compromise or "giving up something in order to get something else." The social worker who is leading the agency policy change effort is constantly attempting to reduce the complexity of the system and the number of surprises. He/she is also allowing for alternatives and deciding if the change goal/idea, or at least part of it, can be achieved and stabilized to benefit clients (Warren, 1977). How to wield power, when to influence, and how to balance control in the change process, are critical elements to think about when attempting agency policy change.

The questions and suggestions that follow are intended to stimulate your thinking as consideration is given to the "who" the social worker plans to bring along to help accomplish the change endeavor. Interested participants begin to emerge during the data collection and analysis activities contained in Components I and II of the Action–Strategy Model. Additional assessment and planning functions carried out by the allies occur in Component III of the Model. Ideas generated by the social worker and allies lead to a discussion of the proper strategy. The change strategy agreed to by the worker and allies propels the effort and development of a preliminary contract to plan implementation of the policy in the agency and/or community. Guidelines, suggestions, and questions are now offered to delineate the steps contained in Component III.

Component III—Develop a Plan of Action Related to the Change Goal/Idea

Identify and Mobilize the Allies

Rally the Allies Within and/or Outside the Agency

List those persons who work in the agency, other human service organizations, or who live in the community and have indicated interest in the policy situation. Eventually, some of these persons will become the "allies."

Are there benefits that will accrue to those who will become involved in changing the policy situation?

When rallying the allies, what type of leadership skills are essential for the social worker to use? Ponder the following questions when rallying the allies.

How does the social worker include those who can be trusted, act interdependently, exercise tolerance, and exert leadership?

How does the social worker exclude those who are opposed to the change idea, but are curious as to the outcome?

How does the social worker balance the idea of "democratic participation" in the allied group while retaining control of the direction of the change effort?

How does the social worker build the motivation, the physical, psychological and intellectual capacities of the allies? And how does he/she increase the opportunities for change?

How does the social worker reconcile differences among the allies, or perhaps between clients/consumers and professional staff, regarding the approach to change? For example, the professional staff may prefer a *rational planning* (goal, objectives formation) or a campaign strategy approach relevant to the change action, but clients/consumers advocate for "social action" or contention tactics.

Assess the Strengths of the Allies

Has the social worker employed a force field analysis to determine restraining and driving forces present in the change effort (Lewin, 1951)?

Are there similar interests indicated by those persons in and outside of the agency about the policy situation?

Are there similar values shared by those persons about the policy situation?

Have those persons who have dissimilar values but an interest in the policy situation been included in the list and asked to share their ideas?

Model Application to Case Example

The example in Chapter 3 contains information about both identifying and rallying the allies in the change effort. Allies within the agency consisted of some concerned staff and some consumers of services. Staff were mobilized by their concern and interest in the policy situation and were then able to identify consumers of the threatened services who might share their concerns. The group, through careful planning, was able to identify and contact potential allies outside the agency who were likely to be particularly influential with the agency Board.

Determine Needs of the Policy Situation

As the social worker and allies try to make some sense of the information that has been gathered and analyzed about the change idea in Component II of the Action–Strategy Model, there is an effort to reduce the number of surprises that will appear on the horizon, such as resistance that swells up in the allies, and opposition from the administration or clients/consumers. The analysis of the policy situation in Component II of the Model provided some general facts about how the agency and clients/consumers could benefit if a policy change was undertaken. Additional questions and answers are required as the process unfolds.

The social worker and allies may be a formal or informal group at this point in the change effort. If it is an informal group, the members will be limited regarding the collection of additional research and data to support the change idea. If the social worker and allies have some clout and are viewed credibly by the decision-making unit or administration, then the allies may be allocated time and money to engage in research in support of the change idea. While there are numerous techniques to conduct research that will assist the allies with reasons as to why or why not the agency policy change will benefit clients/consumers, two approaches are presented here as useful for practitioners.

The first approach, and the more traditional one, is for the social worker and allies to conduct a needs assessment. *Need* is defined as "any identifiable condition that limits a person as an individual or a family member in meeting his or her full potential" (Meenaghan, Washington, & Ryan, 1982, as cited in Netting et al., 1998). A *needs assessment* begins by documenting information about the agency policy, client/consumer needs, the "deficiencies and problems, [and] is still by far the most traveled, and commands the vast majority of our financial human resources" (Kretzman & McKnight, 1993).

There are numerous discussions in social work literature regarding needs assessments (Moroney, 1977; Warheit, Bell, & Schwab, 1977; Meenaghan et al., 1982; Cox et al., 1984, 1987; Kettner et al., 1985; Brody & Nair, 1998; Netting et al., 1998). The purpose of a needs assessment is to document the feasibility for undertaking the proposed agency policy change. Do other workers in the agency think that an agency policy requires change? Are client/consumer needs being addressed by the agency policy according to community standards or norms? Is the need real? Is it perceived to be critical by a particular group either in the human service organization or the community? Has the need evolved during the past several years and has previous documentation been collected? Are there other organizations and communities of similar shape, size, and population, that have moved to address the need in their agencies and community? If so, how and in what way did the process unfold and what happened (Kettner et al., 1985)? The social worker and allies must indicate the type of need in a needs assessment document or report that led them to conclude that an agency policy change is appropriate.

Capacity-Focused Development

The second approach to documenting whether or not there are reasons for an agency policy change is characterized by the phrase, "*capacity-focused development*" (Kretzman & McKnight, 1993). This type of technique is useful in community change and described as an "asset-based community development" approach. The technique reflects the strengths perspective in social work practice with individuals and community organizations (Saleebey, 1997) and asset building in social welfare policy development (Sherraden, 1991). This approach is also closely associated with the concept of empowerment in social work practice, which was discussed earlier in Chapter 3. Empowerment in social work generally refers to "helping to give back a voice to a silenced or disenfranchised client" (Perkins & Tice, in Mandiberg, 2000). A capacity-focused development approach as espoused by Kretzman and McKnight (1993) begins with a "clean commitment" to discovering the assets, resources, and capacities of the agency, its professional staff, and the clients/consumers of the programs and services. The social worker and allies collect data about the assets of the professional staff, the strengths and resources of the clients/consumers and their ability to provide direction for the change effort, and the contributions that can be rendered to the agency if the policy change is implemented. This information, along with the knowledge gained from the analysis undertaken in Component II of the Action–Strategy Model, could subsequently be used to negotiate with the decision-making unit in the agency to prove why an agency policy change may be suitable. Data presented using this technique are based on the positive aspects of the change goal/idea, rather than on deficiencies and problems that exist as a result of identifying unmet needs.

The optimum reasons why agency policy should be changed will be stated in a way that combines a traditional needs assessment with a capacity-focused development, asset-based approach. The body of literature about needs assessments is long-standing and credible. The capacity-focused development, asset-based technique, holds a great deal of promise especially because it focuses on strengths and resources of workers and clients/consumers and integrates with the social work values of self-determination and respect for the innate worth and dignity of all persons. Whatever the approach that is selected, however, it must address the cost of documenting information about the policy change situation in terms of time and money. It must also be executed in a feasible and easily understood manner so that direct service workers, middle management staff, and clients and consumers can make proper use of its content. The following questions need to be answered by the allies in order to be sufficiently prepared to address decisionmakers:

What are the plans of the social worker and allies for determination of the needs of the situation to document the feasibility for undertaking the proposed policy change?

Are clients and consumers part of the allies who will participate in this task?

Has the type of need that has led the social worker and allies to conclude that an agency policy change is appropriate been discussed? For example, is it a survival need or social need or both (Netting et al., 1998)?

What type of needs assessment would the allies utilize if they are attempting to demonstrate feasibility for a proposed agency policy change? For example, would they use a key informant or social indicators approach (Netting et al., 1998)? Perhaps they would use two different needs assessment approaches, such as Delphi techniques (Cox et al., 1987).

Have data about needs or other relevant information that have been gathered about the agency policy change been examined? If so, how can this information be included at this time? How can the allies incorporate statistics, qualitative data, or secondary data in the current needs determination, if these are available?

Will the needs determination generate information about the direction of the effort? How can the social worker and allies best use the information that is generated from the process?

Model Application to Case Example

In the example in Chapter 3, the group attempting to change agency policy used a combination of needs assessment and capacity-focused development. Much necessary information for a needs determination already existed because satisfaction surveys had just been completed within the agency. Through community contacts, the staff involved were also able to collect data about the need to provide respite services to a previously unserved population. They were able to assess potential resources and to present their ideas from a strengths perspective, rather than having emphasis only on what would be lost. They did this by proposing to expand services rather than just save existing, threatened services.

Identify the Target Systems

The group of individuals in an agency or community for whom the agency policy change is aimed constitutes the target systems in the Action–Strategy Model. *Target systems* in the Action–Strategy Model include clients/consumers, higher administration, middle management, professional staff in another community organization, and interested community members. Based on our experiences and the application of the Model, the target systems are divided into *immediate* and *ultimate* target systems as exemplified in Figure 5.1.

The Immediate Target System.   As mentioned earlier, the *immediate target system* consists of the group or groups of individuals in a human service agency who must be convinced that the proposed change idea/goal is desirable and/or necessary. This group exercises power, influence, and control regarding decision making about agency policy and will eventually approve the proposed change. Examples of those persons who make up an immediate target system in a human service agency at the local community level include, but are not limited to, agency boards of directors, advisory committees, client focus groups, clients/consumers, volunteers, sub-committee members, fundraising groups, program managers, clinical supervisors, direct service workers in service units, organizational consultants, and the executive director and his/her planning advisors.

The Ultimate Target System.   The *ultimate target system* consists of the clients/consumers of the agency or persons or groups residing in the community who will benefit directly from the agency policy change. Members of this group may also be part of the immediate target system, such as a client focus group. They may also be part of the allies who have initially become concerned about a policy situation in an agency and who have decided to engage in a change process. Examples of those persons who make up an ultimate target system include, but are not limited to, abused women in a domestic violence shelter, the aged in need of home care, the disabled in an adult foster care setting, and HIV-infected children in foster care. They are often viewed as powerless by professional staff—even by social workers, sadly enough—in the agency and in the community.

Target Systems

Immediate—Board of Directors, Executive Director, Middle-Level Management, Agency Advisory Group

Ultimate— Clients and Consumers of Agency Policy Change

FIGURE 5.1

Following are some questions and suggestions to keep in mind when identifying target systems:

Make a list of persons who constitute the immediate target system associated with the proposed agency policy change in the organization, community, or both. Refer to your organizational charts (formal and informal) that were constructed in Component II of the Action–Strategy Model—the analysis section—as you begin to identify the target systems.

The Immediate Target System

What persons make up the formal aspect of the immediate target system?

What persons make up the informal aspect of the immediate target system?

Are clients/consumers included in the immediate target system? Are they viewed from a strengths- or a problem-focused perspective?

The Ultimate Target System

What persons make up the formal aspect of the ultimate target system?

What persons make up the informal aspect of the ultimate target system?

Identify and Assess the Strengths of Immediate and Ultimate Target Systems. In policy practice the worker and allies have to negotiate with professional staff and administrators before the change idea/goal results in a benefit for the ultimate system—the clients/consumers. Therefore, the social worker and the allies need to determine the motivation, capacity, and opportunity of the immediate target system to approve of the change. They also need to assess the ability of the ultimate target system to engage in the agency policy change, which depends not only on their motivation, capacity, opportunity, and strengths, but also the nature of the change goal/idea.

While many social workers, whose education and training has focused on problem-solving approaches to assist their clients, find it hard to imagine that clients can become part of the solution, we now have intervention models that are certainly a "step up" from the previous disease or pathology models. Recent approaches to social work practice stress solution-focused (DeJong & Miller, 1995), strengths perspective (Saleebey, 1997), personal/community asset-based (Kretzman & McKnight, 1993), and stake-holding (Sherraden, 1991) frameworks of intervention in clinical and policy practice as opposed to traditional problem-focused models. These contemporary approaches emphasize the positive characteristics of persons who are asking for service. In making these assessments of strengths of the immediate and ultimate target systems, the following questions are useful:

Based on past actions and organizational or community history, what is the attitude of the immediate and ultimate target systems regarding agency change in general?

Do the target systems respond to change that emanates from within the agency or community, such as task force recommendations, research studies, client/consumer activities, or volunteer group suggestions?

Do the target systems respond to change that emanates from outside the agency or community, such as regulatory agencies, funding allocations, legislative mandates, court rulings, and client/consumer-oriented recommendations?

Do the target systems desire change? To what degree?

Do the target systems engage in change that is management oriented, a top-down approach; or as in a community decision organization such as the United Way; or is a participatory approach to bring about encouraged change, a bottom-up approach involving staff at all levels?

Do the target systems believe that the proposed agency policy change is worth the time and effort that will be required? What will the agency policy change "do" for the agency or community?

Is the ultimate target system (clients/consumers) viewed by the allies and the immediate target system from a strengths or a problem-focused perspective?

Model Application to Case Example

The social workers and allies in the case example in Chapter 3 were able to identify two immediate targets. They correctly identified that they would need first to convince their own agency board and obtain their approval, before they could ask for funding approval from United Way. The group also identified that their ultimate target consisted of two different client groups, one currently being served by the program, and another that they proposed to serve in an expanded program.

Select an Appropriate Change Strategy

The next step in carrying out the Action–Strategy Model involves the selection of the change strategy that will guide the social worker and allies as they work toward completion of the agency policy change. A *strategy* is defined as the most effective method that the social worker and allies can devise to change agency policy. The selection of the change strategy is dependent on the completion of an accurate analysis of the policy situation including assessment of the strengths and limitations of the allies as well as the immediate and ultimate target systems. Once the appropriate strategy has been chosen, the social worker and allies must decide on specific tactics to implement that strategy. "Strategy shades imperceptibly into tactics" (Cox et al., 1987). *Tactics* are defined as "specific activities designed to elicit a particular response from the target within the context of a discernible strategy" (Homan, 1998). What are the best *means*—political, economic, psychological—that the social worker and allies have at their disposal to bring about the desired agency policy change? The word *means* refers to the choice of tactics to implement the selected strategy. Information that becomes available to the social worker and allies from the needs assessment or capacity development/asset search becomes crucial to the choice of the change strategy and specific tactics. The values held by the social worker and allies and the immediate and ultimate target systems also come into play when choosing a strategy. It is also important to remember that agreement between the social worker and allies and the immediate target system about the agency policy change is not always based on similar values. Occasionally those with differing values will still agree on a particular goal, albeit for different reasons. The immediate and ultimate target system must also be interested in the proposed agency change. *Interest* is formally defined as the "specification of values reflected in actual and potential situations," and as something that "arouses attention" (Warren, 1977). The analytical and assessment components of the agency policy situation, the makeup of the social worker and allies as well as the immediate and ultimate target systems, and the values and interest levels present regarding the proposed agency policy change predict and sometimes dictate the selection of the change strategy and tactics by the social worker and allies.

Useful questions to be asked by the social worker and allies include the following:

Have the social worker and allies used the information gathered in the analysis conducted in Component II of the Action–Strategy Model and the needs determination conducted in Component III to help them select the appropriate change strategy?

What are the best means—political, economic, psychological—that the social worker and allies have at their disposal to bring about the desired agency policy change?

Is there agreement, difference, or dissensus about the agency policy situation between the social worker and allies and the immediate target system?

Is the agency policy change proposed by the social worker and allies less agreeable because it goes against the *interest* of the immediate target system or the ultimate target system?

Is the agency policy change proposed by the social worker and allies less agreeable because it goes against the *values* of the immediate target system, or the ultimate target system?

Is it possible for the social worker and allies to have different value systems than those of the immediate target and ultimate target systems and still work together toward achievement of the agency policy change?

Ideas about definitions and types of change strategies in organizations and communities have been developed in the social work literature throughout the past several decades. Generally included are three categories of change strategies: collaboration, sometimes referred to as cooperation; campaign; and contest or conflict. While there are a multitude of possible tactics associated with each of these strategies, a few are presented in the following discussion.

Cooperation and Collaboration.   When the analysis conducted in Component II and the determination of needs of the policy situation carried out in Component III of the Action–Strategy Model indicate that there is agreement about the need for change regarding the policy situation, and all that is required is to reach agreement on the means for accomplishing the change—a condition described as *issue consensus* (Warren, 1977)—the appropriate strategy choice adopted by the social worker and the allies will be one of *cooperation/collaboration.*

An example of a cooperative/collaborative strategy

An example of a cooperative/collaborative strategy is the initiation of an intake and referral process for a newly established geriatric health screening program by a group of health and social services workers in an aging service agency. The underlying belief is that staff already agree that periodic health screening is beneficial for seniors, but that an intake and referral procedure for the screening is necessary. If there are a few workers who are skeptical, they will, most likely, quickly agree with the thinking of the majority in the group that this type of procedure will make the program run smoothly so that as many seniors as possible can avail themselves of the service. A cooperative/collaborative strategy would lead to approval of the intake and referral process which eventually would benefit the ultimate system of clients/consumers.

Questions to consider in an issue consensus situation when a cooperative/ collaborative strategy is employed include the following:

If agreement about the proposed agency policy change exists and is supported by high values and interest levels, what is the probability that the intervention to change the agency policy will succeed?

What are some tactics that could be used to implement a cooperative/collaborative strategy?

- *Technical, rational, task-oriented planning* (based on the scientific method with a goal and objectives)?
- Organizational self-study?
- Delphi Technique (Cox et al., 1987)?
- Nominal group decision-making approach (Zastrow, 1989)?
- Consensus planning?

What social work roles are played by the social worker and allies?

- *Enabler* (creates a favorable change environment)?
- *Facilitator* (eases the progress of the change process)?
- *Catalyst* (initiates the change effort)?
- *Social Planner* (engages with others and relies on a scientific approach to goal and objectives formation)?

Campaign.   When both the analysis and determination of needs in the policy situation demonstrate that there is no agreement for change, but also indicate that the social worker and allies could win over the opposition with reasonable effort, or at least convince them not to stand in the way of the proposed change—a condition described as *issue difference*—(Warren, 1977), the appropriate strategy choice adopted by the social worker and the allies will be one of *campaign*. Harmony between the values and interest levels of the social worker and allies and the immediate target system is moderate in this environment. It is thought, however, that differences about the goals of the proposed policy change can be worked out. It is hoped that the selection of a campaign strategy will eventually lead to the choice of a cooperation/collaboration strategy to achieve the desired agency policy change. It is noted that campaign strategy is not a terminal strategy but a "transitory phase" that is followed by another strategy. If it is successful then it results in cooperation/collaboration, and if unsuccessful, it could lead to contest (Warren, 1977), or to ending the change effort.

An example of a campaign strategy

An example of a campaign strategy is the development of a research proposal by key administrators and staff in a foster care unit in a family service agency for presentation to the budget committee of the local United Way Board. This activity is demonstrative of an intra-organizational change effort. The purpose of the proposal is to expand the agency training program for foster care parents and to secure the funds necessary to support the effort. The underlying belief is that an expanded training program for foster care parents will help them interact in a more satisfactory manner with the children. The agency administrators and staff of the foster care unit realize that not all members of the United Way budget committee will initially favor the proposal, but it is hoped that they can be persuaded to eventually recommend allocation of the necessary monies to implement the training program.

In an issue difference situation using campaign strategy, the following questions are considered:

If moderate agreement about the proposed agency policy change exists, and it is supported by a mixed combination of values and interest levels, and it is thought that differences about the policy change can be worked out, what is the probability that the intervention to change the agency policy will succeed?

What are some tactics that could be used to implement a campaign strategy?

- Lobbying?
- Testimonials?
- Pledge drives?
- Fact-finding presentations?
- Letter-to-the-Editor campaigns?
- Radio, television, and electronic technology advertising?

What social work roles are played by the social worker and allies?

- Social Planner?
- Expert Witness?
- World Wide Web wizard?
- Broker?

Contest.   When the analysis and determination of needs in the policy situation show that there is no agreement and none is likely to be reached, and the opposition to the proposed change must be defeated if the social worker and allies are to be success-ful—a condition described as *issue dissensus* (Warren, 1977)—then the strategy op-tion adopted by the social worker and allies is one of *contest.* Dissonance rather than harmony between the values and interest levels of the social worker and allies and the immediate target system generally exist in this environment.

Contest is further divided into the two subtypes of *contention* and *conflict.* A strategy of contention, while risky and confrontational in nature, is generally con-ducted within acceptable societal norms, such as a parade or demonstration. Conflict strategy, such as a strike or the use of weapons in connection with the use of force, however, is often outside of acceptable societal norms. Sometimes conflict strategies are illegal and result in bodily and psychological harm to those involved in the effort.

According to Warren (1977),

> Both types of contest by definition seek a goal through the overcoming or defeat of the opposition. But in the case of contention, the chief focus is on the issue, usually on per-suading third parties, in whose hands lies the ultimate outcome, of the superiority of their respective positions. But in cases where third parties are not crucial to the outcome, as well as in some cases where they are, one or both contestants may turn from seeking to win the issue to seeking to harm or destroy the opponent or to remove the opponent from the field of struggle. We reserve the term conflict for this more intense form of contest. It is far less frequent than the other, milder form we call contention.

In an issue dissensus situation when considering a contest strategy some useful questions are:

> If no agreement about the proposed agency policy change exists, and there is no support regarding values and interest levels, and there is little chance of con-vincing decision makers, what is the probability that the intervention to change the agency policy will succeed?

> In this type of environment, the social worker and allies ask themselves the question once again: "Is it worth it?" If the answer is "yes," what is the appro-priate strategy selection: contention or conflict?

An example of a contention strategy

An example of a contention strategy is the circulation of a petition by direct service workers to establish a "smoke-free" environment in the client/consumer waiting room in their agency. The underlying belief is that a "smoke-free" environ-ment is healthy for everyone in the agency. The workers previously attempted to per-suade the administration that this kind of environment is desirable for all persons in the organization—clients/consumers and staff alike—but to no avail. So, staff are left with the idea that the opposition must be defeated. While the circulation of a pe-tition is risky, and may be confrontational and coercive in nature, it is within accept-able societal norms and will not result in physical harm to the immediate target system. If circulation of the petition nets adequate signatures and is presented to agency managers and directors, then it could result in victory for the direct service workers and a defeat for the administration. It could result in defeat for the direct service workers, however. In this example, the Board of Directors (third party) would most likely make the final decision. The social worker and allies may even attempt to influence the Board of Directors. A third party usually makes the decision regarding the outcome of this type of policy situation because a decision cannot be reached by the parties involved.

An example of a conflict strategy

An example of a conflict strategy is the initiation of a media smear campaign by direct service workers, directed at the administration about a policy situation that they think is legally and socially unjust for clients/consumers of the agency—mandatory fingerprinting of all applicants who apply for public assistance benefits in a county welfare office. The underlying belief is that when clients are fingerprinted this is an invasion of their privacy and an attack on their civil rights. The strategies of cooperation and campaign have been attempted by the service workers, and have failed. A conflict strategy of this type is very risky because it falls outside of acceptable societal norms and could easily result in psychological harm to all involved. For openers, the direct service workers will risk being fired from their jobs, or being asked to resign. The outcome in this type of policy situation is also usually decided by a third party such as an executive board, a court, a fact-finding task force, or even the state legislature. The social worker and allies and the immediate target system cannot reach agreement regarding the outcome of the policy situation and it is decided by an outside or third party.

In an issue dissensus situation when contemplating whether contention or conflict strategies are appropriate, some questions to consider include the following:

Contention

If a contention strategy is used, are the social worker and allies willing to submit their agency policy change to a "third party," such as a mediator, arbitrator, or an outside authority?

What are some tactics that could be used to implement a strategy of contention?

- Petition circulation?
- Legislative debates?
- Sit-in and sick-in protests?
- Informational picketing?

What social work roles are played by the social worker and allies?

- Advocate?
- Social action organizer?
- *Contestant* (someone who deliberately challenges and coerces those opposed to the change effort)?

Conflict

If a strategy of conflict is employed, are the social worker and allies willing to eliminate the opposition by such means as recall and efforts to remove someone from a position of power in the agency?

What are some tactics that could be used to implement a strategy of conflict?

- Boycotts?
- Illegal strikes such as law enforcement, public school employees, air traffic controllers have used in similar situations?
- Brainwashing?
- Media and electronic technology smear campaigns?
- Use of physical violence and weapons?

What social work roles are played by the social worker and allies?

- Contestant?
- Protestor?
- Advocate?

To finalize your thinking in the selection of the appropriate strategy, consider Figure 5.2 that lists some advantages and disadvantages of cooperation/collaboration and contest. Note that campaign strategy is not included, because it is not a terminal strategy. It is expected that it will be followed by another strategy which, if successful, is usually collaboration/cooperation.

Model Application to Case Example

The case presented in Chapter 3 is a good example of campaign strategy choice. It was clear to the group hoping to accomplish change that issue differences were present. They felt that consensus already existed among direct service staff, but not among administrative staff. Their assessment of the situation, however, led them to believe that they could very likely persuade other staff and the Board of Directors. In this situation, a strategy choice of contest was not really feasible, even if it had been called for. If it did not appear likely that they could persuade the Director and Board of Directors, it would have required an attempt to have them removed/replaced. This did not appear to be a viable choice.

Develop a Preliminary Contract for Implementation of Agency Policy Change

At this point in the evaluation of the steps in the Action–Strategy Model, the change process is still in the experimental stage. The social worker and allies need some form of validation regarding their ideas. Similar to the activities of the researcher who conducts a scientific experiment and pre-tests a survey instrument to determine reliability and validity, the social worker and allies pre-test their idea about the

CHANGE STRATEGIES

Cooperation/Collaboration

Advantages	Disadvantages
Results advantageous to everyone in community Outcome superior to any one outcome proposed System affirmed People less likely to oppose change, more likely will be stabilized All are winners Cooperation has tendency to escalate	Changes in existing system itself is difficult with this method Results modified through cooperation so that original goals sometime not really met

Contention		Conflict	
Advantages	*Disadvantages*	*Advantages*	*Disadvantages*
Contention activity can strengthen allies if not taken too far Clarify issues Can strengthen larger system if it does not go too far (Some groups seeking destruction of larger system may not see this as relevant) Does not threaten viability of existing system	Can weaken allies if methods become too radical Social workers as change agents can be coopted by system they are trying to change Contention may escalate into conflict and may cause loss of control by allies and loss of opportunity for favorable outcomes	Conflict activity can strengthen allies if not taken too far Can reduce tension and clarify issues through conflict resolution Can strengthen larger system if it does not go too far (Some groups seeking destruction of larger system may not see this as relevant) Threatens viability of existing system	Can weaken allies if methods become too radical Social workers as change agents can be coopted by system they are trying to change

FIGURE 5.2

agency policy change to determine its reliability and validity. They must be able to explain not only how the policy needs to be changed and why (based on the determination of needs), but what the implementation of the change would entail. Even though the Model presented in this text does not cover actual implementation of the policy change, a thoroughly developed plan for implementation will be an asset in acquiring approval when proposing the agency change to decision makers; in fact, it sometimes can be the deciding factor.

    The social worker and allies must anticipate what questions will be asked and be prepared to answer them. They are seeking consensus in the immediate target system that the agency policy change should be implemented. Weinbach (1998) relates that contracting is "a special kind of cooperation with the task environment." Earlier in this text in Chapter 1, the "task environment" was referred to as the agency in the environment concept. Netting, Kettner, and McMurtry (1998) define the "task environment" as those "external organizations on which an organization depends, either as providers of needed input (money, raw materials, client referrals) or as consumer of its output." Contracting occurs with those parts of an organization that have the ability to set goals and seek their attainment. In the Action–Strategy Model, the task environment for the worker and allies is usually the immediate target system such as the Board of Directors, or an agency advisory committee. A contract is a promise between the allies and the immediate target system that certain things will happen. It can be formal, explicit, and in writing. It can be informal, implicit with a verbal statement of agreement or a handshake between a member of the allies and a member of the immediate target system. An implicit contract is usually based more on trust between the allies and immediate target system and may be appropriate depending on the nature of the agency policy change, the size of the agency, and the characteristics of the ultimate target system. Although the contract may be an informal one, the same questions that are contained in a formal contract need to be addressed. The most important characteristic of the contract is the idea that there is accountability built into the process to ensure that the agency policy change is implemented. Contracts are widely used in social work practice and range from therapeutic ones to consultation services by experts for a service development or a training program for staff.

    One effective method of "thinking through" all the steps necessary to successfully implement the change is to develop a *preliminary contract* for implementation. This activity will eventually become the basis for the negotiation of the final contract between the social worker and allies that takes place in Component IV, the final process of the Action–Strategy Model.

    As the social worker and allies think through exactly what steps would be required in order for the agency policy change to be implemented, and decide what time lines would be necessary for these steps to be carried out effectively, they will also be carefully identifying the persons who would need to be responsible for each task stated. A preliminary contract is a tool for facilitating the thought process necessary for implementation of the agency policy change. For example, if one identifies as a necessary task for implementing a particular policy change the provision of a training session of the changes for all staff, then the contract would spell out who would conduct the training session, by what date the training would be completed, and how the effectiveness of the training would be measured. It would also spell out who would be responsible for preparing or purchasing the training materials, and who would make all the logistical arrangements for the training location. The benefit of developing such a contract **prior** to obtaining approval of the agency policy change is that the presenters of the policy change are much better prepared to explain exactly what would be required for implementation, and to realistically answer questions about probable expenditures of agency resources for the implementation. A second benefit is that, once approval is obtained, the preliminary contract becomes the base on which to develop the final contract, by simply incorporating any changes required or recommended by the decision makers.

Three basic tasks are associated with establishing a contract for an agency policy change: identify the goal, state the objectives, and tie the objectives to measurement and outcome. Useful questions for each task are as follows:

Identify the Goal

Where have we been (social worker and allies) and where are we going?

Has an appropriate change strategy been selected that will guide us with the plan for the implementation of the agency policy change?

Has an outcome been projected based on the selection of a change strategy?

What parties will be involved in the preliminary contract? Immediate target system? Ultimate target system?

What is there about the policy situation that is most critical, feasible, and likely to succeed, as assessed by the social worker and allies, and as viewed by the immediate target system?

What are the barriers or resistance to change in the policy situation?

State the Goal

What is the outcome that the social worker and allies desire?

Can the outcome be rephrased as a goal statement?

Is the goal specific to the policy situation?

Identify the Objectives

How can the goal be achieved?

What are the means that will be used by the social worker and allies to achieve the goal?

State the Objectives

What are the objectives that can be spelled out in clear, behavioral terms?

Are the objectives specific to and reflective of the goal statement?

Tie the Objectives to Measurement and Outcome

Who are the agency staff who will approve the outcome or the result of the agency policy change?

Who are the clients/consumers who will be the ultimate target of the outcome—the agency policy change?

What is the date by which time the objectives will be completed?

If the objectives are carried out, will the goal become an outcome or result?

What standards will be established to evaluate the agency policy change process and the goal achievement?

Who will evaluate the agency policy change process and the goal achievement?

What research methods will be used throughout the evaluation? Quantitative, qualitative, or a combination of approaches?

Whenever possible, preliminary contracts must spell out, in clear behavioral terms, the responsibilities in the agreement. Those responsibilities must be set in a time frame and must be stated in measurable terms. Two different approaches to goal statements are now presented.

1. ABC Agency staff will work on improving their attitudes toward AIDS clients/ consumers.
2. In order to improve attitudes toward AIDS clients/consumers, ABC Agency staff will participate in no less than three training sessions on working with AIDS clients/consumers within the next six months. Attitudes will be measured by use of pre- and post-tests given before the first training session, and again at the end of the last training session. The agency will contract for the training sessions with the HIV/AIDS Community Training Council. Pre- and post-tests will be administered and results will be interpreted by the Greater Lakes Evaluation Center. An increase of at least 50 percent in understanding and acceptance of AIDS clients/consumers by the agency staff will be considered an indication of success.

Obviously, the second approach is superior to the first one and could be used in the development of a preliminary contract. Signature lines for every person identified in the contract who has a responsibility would also be included. If a responsible party consists of a number of staff—too many to identify individually, such as agency line staff—then someone who has the authority to ensure that those persons carry out their responsibilities, such as supervisors, will be identified in the contract as having the task of ensuring that staff complete those identified responsibilities. In that situation, the supervisors would have signature lines. Another alternative, when there is unanimous agreement by line staff, would be to have a staff person, designated by the other staff, sign on behalf of the entire staff. For accountability purposes, it is generally better for supervisors to sign, because continuity of staff cannot be guaranteed, and the addition of new staff can alter the unanimous nature of the agreement. The exception to this, of course, would be if the staff belong to a union or other agency organization, which had the authority to sign agreements on behalf of staff. Again, every person who has a responsibility identified in the contract has a signature line that includes a date space, and no one has a signature line who does not have identified responsibilities.

Model Application to Case Example

The case example in Chapter 3 indicates that the social workers and allies made extensive preparations for their presentation to the Board of Directors. In anticipation of board member questions, they went through the steps that would be required to implement their recommendations as they prepared. This process is, in effect, the development of a preliminary contract. In their effort to gain approval for the agency policy change, they also prepared a suggested contract proposal.

Develop a Plan for Evaluation of Agency Policy Change

The task of formulating a preliminary contract leads to the development of a plan for evaluating the agency policy change. While it is not our purpose to discuss various research designs and evaluation approaches in the field of social welfare policy, we stress that **accountability, and evaluation of social work interventions, is critical for the survival of our profession**. Some ideas about how an agency policy change can be evaluated are briefly presented in the next several paragraphs.

Evaluation of the Plan Is Ongoing Throughout the Implementation of the Change. A plan for *evaluation* means that the social worker and allies attach a value to the steps that will take place during the implementation. This plan is the design regarding how each step in the implementation will be reviewed and checked from beginning to end and beyond the end—to the impact it has on the quality of life for clients/consumers. The allies need feedback to keep their level of motivation high. They need to stop, look, listen, and assess the signals that appear as they plan for the implementation of the agency policy change. The following questions are useful as the allies plan the evaluation process:

> Have the social worker and allies consistently realized that the right to intervene to make changes in the way other people lead their lives is an awesome responsibility?

> Have the social worker and allies consistently completed each step and each task in Components I, II, and III of the Model in the best possible manner and in accordance with the Code of Ethics?

> Have the social worker and allies consistently asked at the end of each step in Components I, II, and III of the Action–Strategy Model of Agency Policy Change: "Do we think that we can move forward with the policy situation?" and "Is it worth it?"

> Have the social worker and allies formulated the preliminary contract so that it serves not only as the plan for action but the basis of the evaluation process in a behaviorally specific manner with feasible goals and objectives?

Model Application to Case Example

While not spelled out in the case example in Chapter 3, a plan for evaluation was included in the presentation to the agency Board of Directors. The social workers and allies presented a draft funding proposal for United Way, and a draft contract for Community Mental Health. Both of those documents, of necessity, contained detailed evaluation plans. Because extensive data and information had been gathered by the group, both within the agency and in the community, development of plans for ongoing and final evaluation were not difficult.

Final Measurement Follows Implementation of the Change.   An evaluation plan depends on clearly stated criteria to be monitored and followed by the social worker and the allies. This is sometimes referred to as *proactive evaluation*, a deliberate method of keeping track of the change process from one step to the next, rather than waiting until the action has ceased and then trying to remember everything that happened, which is sometimes referred to as *reactive evaluation*. The social worker and allies, of course, must adopt a proactive stance to avoid pitfalls, conduct alternative planning, reduce barriers, and eliminate undesirable consequences in the policy situation. Clearly stated criteria are recognized as the goals and objectives, time frame, and responsibility taking that were agreed to by the allies and target systems as discussed in the preliminary contract phase of the Action–Strategy Model, and dictate who is to be held accountable and how the agency policy change will be implemented. The size of the agency policy change, the strength and resources of the allies, the ability of the target systems—immediate and ultimate—to be brought along in the process, and the chosen strategy all predict the breadth and depth of the plan of evaluation. The plan of evaluation may simply consist of a designated person collecting and reviewing notes about completion of activities on a daily basis and then writing a report for the immediate target system.

The plan, however, may consist of an elaborate research design replete with goal statements, various types of objectives, numerical data, and computer software programs to process descriptive information and spew out inferential statistics. After all, an intervention has been proposed that will result in agency policy change. It behooves the social worker and allies to devise a way to measure the progress and result of this intervention. This is sometimes referred to as impact evaluation that measures the effectiveness of the agency policy change. This means that the social worker and allies figure out how to evaluate the progress or lack thereof regarding the change, as well as its effectiveness, or sacrifice and relinquish that responsibility to someone else. Again, these ideas relate to the accountability of the social worker and allies engaged in agency policy change. Remember that the agency policy change has not been implemented at this stage of the game, but the immediate target system must be informed about how the impact of the agency policy change will be evaluated if it is to be implemented.

Two important questions to be considered are presented.

Have the social worker and allies planned to execute a *summative* evaluation study that includes all data and final outcomes to judge the process and the result of the agency policy change after it has been implemented (Kettner et al., 1985)?

Have the social worker and allies recognized and addressed issues of diversity, injustice, and discrimination that have affected the social worker and allies and the immediate and ultimate target systems throughout the change effort, as well as the result of the agency policy change after it has been implemented?

Develop a Plan for Stabilization of Agency Policy Change

Stabilization means that a newly created agency policy or the expansion and improvement of an existing one is securely intact as an integral part of agency life. It has been approved and accepted by the immediate target system, which usually consists of the administration and a Board of Directors or an Executive Board. Stabilization assures that the agency policy change will take its place in a credible location in the agency, the agency manual or operating procedural rules. It affirms that staff have been directed regarding its implementation on behalf of clients/consumers of the agency. It also assures that the necessary resources are present and forthcoming and that the change has been implemented in such a manner that it can withstand the onslaught of internal or external forces that may thwart the overall effort (Warren, 1977; Kettner et al., 1985). The process of stabilization corresponds with Lewin's theory about the final stage of the change process, that is, the "freezing on the new level" (Lewin, 1951). This stage is also referred to as "refreezing." According to Weick and Quinn (1999), "Refreezing that embeds the new behavior and forestalls relapse is most likely to occur when the behavior fits both the personality of the target and the relational expectations of the target's social network."

There must be a plan for stabilization of the change if it is to take place. The plan is contingent on the successful completion of all phases in Components I, II, and III of the Action–Strategy Model, especially the determination of needs and change strategy selection. The stabilization plan must contain information about how the ultimate target system—clients/consumers—will benefit from the agency policy change once it has been implemented. The plan is also dependent on the value of and interest in the policy situation, the size of the agency policy change, the strength and limitations of the social worker and the allies, the receptiveness of the immediate target system, the chosen strategy, the construction of the preliminary contract, and the plan for evaluation. The social worker and allies must also give thought to the idea that they do not possess personal ownership of the new or improved agency policy. The plan for stabilization often involves the withdrawal of those who originally brought about the change so that the goal that has been achieved can stand on its own merits. The aim of the plan for stabilization is to solidify the change (Warren, 1977). Several important questions come to mind.

Have the social worker and allies determined for themselves what was initially of importance to them regarding the agency policy situation?

Have the social worker and allies respected the rights and interests of the clients/consumers of the organization regarding the agency policy situation?

Have the social worker and allies determined whether clients or consumers of the agency would improve in some way as a result of the agency policy change?

Have the social worker and allies determined whether the agency policy change was practical and ethical?

Have the social worker and allies determined whether the agency policy change would be measured qualitatively through reports and record keeping, or quantitatively through the collection and interpretation of statistical data, or both?

Have the social worker and allies determined how the preceding information (evaluation) would be distributed to staff throughout the agency?

Have the social worker and allies planned for the provision and continuation of resources so that the agency policy change would become secure after the initial implementation?

Have the social worker and allies planned for their eventual withdrawal from the change process by preparing other professional staff to carry out and carry on the agency policy change?

Have the social worker and allies attempted whenever possible to bring the client/consumer population along in the decision-making process so that they, too, would value and benefit from the agency policy change?

Have the social worker and allies recognized and dealt with issues of diversity, injustice, and discrimination potentially contained in the agency policy change that could affect its stabilization?

Have the social worker/allies discussed ideas to "buffer" the agency policy change "against external intervention that might wipe it out" (Warren, 1977)?

Model Application to Case Example

In the case example, the professional staff recommended to their board not only to continue the Home Help & Respite Care Program but to expand that to provide services for the developmentally disabled. The board, excited by the prospect of collaborating with the United Way Funding Board and the director of Community Mental Health, eventually approved the request of the staff and asked that the director draft a contract that would become the basis for the implementation of the plan. Although not detailed in the case example, the contract would provide form and structure to the process and ensure that stabilization of the policy change would most likely take place.

Develop a Plan for Eliminating or Decreasing Effects of Resistance and Undesirable Consequences

Just as important as the plan for implementation, evaluation, and stabilization is the development of a plan to deal with the inevitable resistance to the implementation of the agency policy change. After developing a change proposal, it may be tempting to assume that there will be no resistance to implementation of that change. Even when there is uniform agreement on the need for the change, a plan for countering resistance is necessary. Because change is implemented by humans, and because humans tend to revert to familiar ways of doing things, even if they intellectually agree things need to be done differently, resistance will creep in. Anyone who has ever tried to change their eating habits or adopt a new lifestyle will understand this concept.

While developing a plan for countering resistance, one must also plan for undesirable consequences. This will require the ability and willingness to imagine all of the possible outcomes of implementation beyond the focus of intended outcomes. Because agency policy change is often being implemented in complex systems, anticipation of all possible outcomes may not be possible. However, the social worker and allies have an obligation to anticipate as many as possible, and to develop a plan for decreasing the effects of or eliminating the undesirable ones. Here are some questions that are based on concepts of resistance discussed earlier in Chapter 4 to consider as you complete the final steps in Component III of the Model:

> Has the problem of **habit** interfered with the efforts of the social worker/allies regarding effecting the agency policy change?
>
> Has the situation of "let's not rock the boat" to avoid **disruption** limited the change efforts of the social worker and allies?
>
> Have **vested interests** or self-serving actions interfered with the activities of the social worker and allies, especially regarding negotiations in the contract phase with the immediate target system?
>
> Has **ideology**, such as adopting an incremental approach to change rather than a conflict or radical one, threatened the progress of the social worker and allies, especially regarding the formation of the allies and the development of the preliminary contract?
>
> Have the social worker and allies adopted **irrational reactions** to change ideas and efforts during any stage and phase of the change effort and voiced negative opinions about the agency policy change?
>
> Have the social worker and allies brainstormed about all of the possible outcomes, negative and positive, regarding the implementation of the agency policy change?
>
> Have the social worker and allies attempted to anticipate the consequences of the outcome and developed a plan to decrease the undesirable ones?

Model Application to Case Example

The overall goal of the professional staff at the Child and Family Service Agency, developing a plan of action to convince their Board that an existing policy could be revised and expanded, was accomplished. Resistance, however, can always rear its ugly head at any time throughout any change process. Actual implementation of the agency policy change including carrying out the specifications contained in the contract, writing a funding proposal for submission to the United Way Board, and ensuring the continued support of the Community Mental Health Director, looms in the future. While not discussed in the case example in Chapter 3, the professional staff must further plan to make certain that the change will actually take place and that resistance and interference will be eliminated or at least kept to a minimum. This activity is best undertaken when enthusiasm abounds and the social worker and allies can sustain the momentum gained from their recent success.

Summary

The Action–Strategy Model is appealing because it is a plan of action that can be applied and executed by the social worker and allies and clients/consumers of the proposed change. Motivation to engage in the planning process is based on the belief that the agency policy change is valued and beneficial to clients/consumers. Also critical are the level of interest and the saliency of the policy situation.

The execution of the Action–Strategy Model is dependent on the policy situation, the change idea that eventually becomes a change goal, the make-up of the allies, the determination of needs, the composition of the target systems—immediate and ultimate—and the change strategy. Content in Chapter 6 focuses on the steps that are required to move the planning process forward into the implementation stage in order to accomplish the agency policy change.

Important Terms and Phrases _____

Allies
Benefits
  instrumental
  expressive
Capacity-focused development
Contestant
Evaluation
  proactive
  reactive
  summative
Force field analysis
Interest
Issue consensus
Issue differences
Issue dissensus
Means
Need
Needs assessment
Plan
Preliminary contract

Rational
Rational planning
Social work roles
  enabler
  facilitator
  catalyst
  social planner
Stabilization
Strategy
  cooperation and collaboration
  campaign
  contest–contention
  conflict
Tactics
Target systems
  immediate
  ultimate
Task-oriented planning
Technical

Learning Exercises

1. Select a human service organization/agency with which you are very familiar. If you are in field placement, you should select your placement agency.

    For the selected agency, draw an organizational chart that represents the formal structure of the agency. Draw this chart to the best of your knowledge. When you have finished, you should be able to determine the official flow of decision making, or the "chain of command."

    Next, think about that organization and how things "really" get done. Consider whom people go to when they want to know where something is; or how to get supplies ordered; or how to "shortcut" the official system when you are in a hurry. Also consider who socializes with whom at lunchtime; who golfs with whom. After reflecting on the informal system of the agency, draw a chart that illustrates the working of this informal structure.

    After completion of both charts, compare them and analyze both similarities and differences.

2. Imagine that you are a social worker in a family service agency, located in a mid-size city. Some of the services provided by your agency include family counseling and parent support groups. Especially helpful to many families has been parent education classes, a series held at your agency, but whose classes are taught by professionals from your agency, the local Health Department, and the local Child Guidance Clinic of Community Mental Health. In addition, your agency has been host, for the last two years, to a Child Welfare Awareness Fair, which is held twice a year. The entire agency building is available to any community agency concerned with child welfare issues for a day-long public education/parent information effort. Display tables and booths are available and refreshments are served. Almost all community agencies have participated and these events have been considered very successful and beneficial. You are concerned about the lack of family services available for parents who work during the day. Your agency, for example, is currently open during typical business hours only, and all services provided at your agency occur during that time period.

    Using the Strategy Chart, on page 102, develop an imaginary policy change proposal that addresses this concern. List some of the tactics you would employ in a collaboration strategy at the organization level. Then list some of the tactics you would employ if you were using a campaign strategy and then a contest strategy at the organizational level. In listing tactics, try to be descriptive and realistic. As an example, for campaign strategy you might identify "Letter writing blitz to the local newspaper."

    Next, imagine that you are attempting to accomplish the same change, but as it relates to the agencies involved in the parent education series, or inter-organizational level. Now list tactics for each of the three strategies for this level of change.

    Finally, imagine that you are attempting this same change, but at the level of the whole community. Imagine that you not only want the Child Welfare Awareness Fair to accommodate the schedules of working parents, but that you want all community agencies to become more responsive to this issue at their agencies. Again, list tactics for each of the three strategies for change at a community level.

STRATEGY CHART

Agency Policy Change

Immediate Target Systems	Change Strategies		
	Cooperation (Collaboration)	*Campaign*	*Contest*
Agency	1. 2. 3.		
Inter-Organization(s)			
Community (Or part of a community)			

Study Questions _____

1. What is the difference between instrumental and expressive benefits?

2. Why do you think that it is important to identify and mobilize the "allies" in the effort to change agency policy?

3. When documenting the need for an agency policy change, what is the difference between using a needs assessment approach and a capacity-focused development approach?

4. In the case example presented in Chapter 3, who is the immediate target and who is the ultimate target?

5. Given the political and economic climate of today's world of social welfare organization—public, nonprofit, or for-profit—what change strategy discussed in Chapter 5 seems most appropriate for use by direct service social workers who are attempting agency policy change? Why?

6. What are the benefits of developing a preliminary contract?

7. Why does the plan for evaluating an agency policy change need to include on-going evaluation as well as a final evaluation?

8. What purpose would be served by developing a plan for stabilization of an agency policy change?

6

Explanation and Application of the Model

Component IV

Goal Statement

To demonstrate how the fourth component of the Action–Strategy Model, Implement the Change Strategy to Accomplish Approval of the Agency Policy Change, can be used by the social worker and allies as they complete tasks and take deliberate action to implement their change strategy to affect agency policy change.

Discussion

You can't change the world in four hundred ways. Maybe two or three, however. Let's make those count.—BSW Student, 1993

Component I of the Action–Strategy Model invites social workers to dream about a better way that clients/consumers could be served in a human service agency. Component II is concerned with the analysis of the agency policy situation, the determination of a feasible change goal/idea, identification of undesirable consequences and resistance to change, and the creation of a working hypothesis about the policy situation. We can view Components I and II and their sub-parts as "conditions before" the intervention takes place. We measure these conditions in a qualitative manner, mostly through written analyses that have been prepared by the social worker and allies.

Component III of the Model lays out the plan of action of the intervention aimed at the immediate target system. It includes the identification of the allies and target systems, determination of the need, selection of the change strategy, development of a preliminary contract with goals and objectives, and a plan for evaluation and stabilization of the agency policy change. The activities in Component III of the Model are action steps even though the actual implementation of the plan has not yet taken place and can also be measured using qualitative methods.

Component IV, Implementing the Change Strategy to Accomplish Change, is predominately characterized by the finalization of a contract for the implementation of the agency policy change. It contains specific steps that the allies carry out while using their chosen strategy: cooperation/collaboration, campaign, contention, or conflict. The idea here is that if the steps in Component IV are followed and implemented, then the immediate target system will provide positive feedback and officially approve the agency policy change—the last part of the process. As you will recall, the immediate target system consists of decision makers whom the allies hope to influence. While direct service staff work with others to bring about change in agency policy, they rarely have the ability to authorize it. Middle management or higher administrative units generally have this power. Evaluation takes place at all stages and phases of the evolution of the Model. The final outcome of the change effort is measured by impact and summative evaluations that assess the value of the policy change in the ultimate target system—the clients/consumers of the agency.

Component IV—Implement the Change Strategy to Accomplish Approval of the Agency Policy Change

Evaluate and Adjust for Resistance and Undesirable Consequences

As the allies are engaged in using their chosen strategy to accomplish the proposed change, they must constantly be on the lookout for resistance. Keep in mind that while resistance can occur during any phase of the execution of the Action–Strategy Model, it is more likely to happen during the implementation of the change strategy phase of the process where the real work of change takes place.

The adopted strategy helps the allies reach their goal. Despite the fact that an appropriate strategy has been chosen, or even one that is mostly acceptable with some adaptations, something may happen that stops allies in their tracks. For instance, a loss of control may occur for a short time while another individual or group decides what the course of action will be. The implementation of the chosen strategy in relation to the change goal/idea will either assist or deter the allies from reaching that goal. If the strategy is one of cooperation/collaboration or campaign, the greater the possibility to achieve the goal, albeit with some adjustment to the objectives. If the strategy is one of contention or conflict, the less likely the allies will reach their goal and a third party will be called on to make the decision. The choice of strategy that was agreed to in Component III of the Model is a crucial factor in the change process.

The steps discussed in Component IV of the Model in this section of the chapter are primarily reflective of the change strategies of collaboration and campaign. There are circumstances in which the strategies of contention and conflict are appropriate and result in successful outcomes, such as the social protest actions of the members of the disabled and gay populations and class action lawsuits brought about by state attorneys general against tobacco companies. There are also times when contention and conflict strategies are necessary to draw attention to an issue. Society can always benefit from a few good radicals to stir up the pot of social conditions that contains social injustices and discrimination. Today's world of policy making does not lend itself as easily to contention and conflict strategies as it did in the times of social upheaval in the 1960s. Change strategies that focus on the reduction of conflict and controversy are in vogue in the current world of social welfare policy. Collaboration and cohesiveness are the buzzwords of community decision makers as they engage in change in social welfare systems at the local level. Social workers who engage in agency policy change need to realize this. Before considering some tactics associated with collaboration and campaign strategies to implement an agency policy change consider the following questions:

> Has the chosen strategy—cooperation/collaboration, campaign, or contest— propelled the social worker and allies into the implementation stage of seeking approval for the agency policy change as based on the goal and objectives contained in the preliminary contract?
>
> Are the social worker and allies predicting that the agency policy change will be simple to accomplish, that resistance to its approval from the immediate target system is low or non-existent, and that a cooperative/collaborative strategy will work throughout the process?
>
> Are the social worker and allies predicting that the agency policy change will evoke differences in the immediate target system regarding its approval, that there will be some resistance to the change, but the resistance will be decreased through a campaign strategy to achieve approval?
>
> Are the social worker and allies predicting that the agency policy change will create differences in the immediate target system that are incompatible and contrary to its substance, that there is total resistance that cannot be decreased, and that a contest strategy will be selected to coerce the immediate target system to implement the change?
>
> What degree of stabilization regarding the agency policy change is predicted by the social worker and allies if resistance in the immediate target system is low, medium, or high?

Model Application to Case Example

In the case example in Chapter 3, the staff employed a campaign strategy that included gathering data, conducting a needs assessment, and advancing ideas and information to interested persons and leaders in the community. Eventually, they were able to persuade the Director of Community Mental Health as well as their own

Board of Directors and agency director that their ideas were valid and feasible. Familiarity with and knowledge of the agency, its task environment, and the community led to the selection of a campaign strategy. As staff implemented this strategy, they were eventually able to collaborate to achieve consensus about their plan for the agency policy change. Data collection and needs assessments carried out during steps in Component III of the Model contained information that was used to anticipate questions to address areas of concern and resistance to the change idea from decision makers. The point is that staff must continually evaluate their actions in the change process. Constant anticipation of resistance and consistent evaluation of effort throughout allow the social worker and staff to predict with a fair degree of certainty that the agency policy can be accomplished.

Methods of Presenting Proposed Change to Decision Makers

Social workers are often invited to present and discuss programs and services to community decision makers for the purpose of providing information about innovative approaches to service delivery and creative opportunities for clients/consumers. Several types of presentations are discussed that may be used at this stage of the Model.

Use of Position Papers.   In this text, the idea is advanced that the social worker and allies can use position papers in three different ways. The first approach is to use a position paper that has already been issued by a credible organization, such as the National Association of Social Workers or the Child Welfare League of America, to attract attention to a particular agency policy situation and to support an agency policy change. For example, the publication, *Social Work Speaks* (2000), contains numerous position statements of interest to social workers that focus on social welfare policies. In this instance, a position paper generates interest in the policy change as well as educating the immediate target system about its significance. A position paper that is used as part of a presentation can also be aimed at convincing the target system about the efficacy of an agency policy change. It is useful in campaign and contest situations. It is also beneficial as a collaborative technique, however, where agreement on a goal exists, but the social worker and allies are still attempting to reach consensus/agreement on methods to reach the goal.

This text is not intended to provide comprehensive information on how to write a position paper, but rather to help you understand what a position paper is and how you can utilize one in your presentation. According to Donald Lathrop (n.d.), in his work entitled *The Preparation and Use of Position Statements in Social Work Practice*, "position statements are used to consolidate and express organizational or group views on public issues and public social policy. . . . Each such statement provides a collective voice on matters of mutual concern." A position paper or statement is, therefore, a stand taken on an issue, by a legitimate organization, and is widely disseminated, generally to a broad audience. The position taken represents the public interest, or the common good, rather than promoting a specific benefit to the issuing organization. It is clear then that the direct service staff of a particular agency would not issue a position paper recommending better pay and benefits for themselves. That would clearly be self-serving and not be promoting the common good. The staff of that agency might, however, issue a position paper recommending that direct service staff of all agencies, as a group, receive better pay and benefits. Such a statement would need to show how such an action would benefit society in general, and clients/consumers in particular.

What kinds of organizations and groups generally issue position papers or statements? According to the Lathrop article, professional membership organizations, deliberative bodies or assemblies, conferences, committees, advisory boards, councils, chapters, governing boards, agency staffs, faculties, student organizations, and professional groups all may take a stand on a public issue by writing such a document (Lathrop, n.d.).

The social worker and allies will need to locate a position statement made on a topic that is relevant to the policy change they are proposing. While it would be helpful if a position statement had been issued supporting or recommending the particular type of policy being proposed, one that presents the issue in a more general way can still be very useful. For example, let us say that the social worker and allies, in a sexual assault agency, are proposing a policy change to the board that would expand the eligibility criteria for group counseling services to include adolescent perpetrators, a heretofore unserved group for the agency. A position paper that supports any efforts to remediate problems for this population, on the belief that it would prevent future sexual assault and domestic violence, could be a very convincing addition to the presentation. Of particular importance is the identity of the group or organization issuing the position paper. In the preceding example, a position paper developed and issued by the agency staff would not be nearly as convincing or lend as much credibility to the argument as would one issued by a professional organization. It is important that the issuing body not only be recognizable to the decision makers, but that it be credible and palatable. For example, if one is attempting to convince the Board of Directors of an agency supported primarily by Catholic religious groups, then quoting a position statement issued by a pro-choice organization is probably not helpful.

When referring to the position paper in the presentation, it is important to quote enough to give your proposed policy change credibility, and to show how this organization's position in fact supports such a policy. Two or three sentences generally will accomplish this. Do not attempt to incorporate the entire position statement, unless it is very brief and the entire statement is relevant. Be sure to identify the issuing organization and the date the position was issued. For example, one might say: "On January 10, 2001, the American Association of Retired Persons (AARP) issued a position paper on the importance of a full continuum of services being available to the elderly poor. Within that paper they make the following statement . . ." and so on.

How does one locate a position paper? A credible beginning place would be the library and the world wide web. It is also helpful to contact key organizations that would be likely to issue position papers, and ask them if they have issued such a paper/statement on a topic relevant to your policy change. Some questions to consider when the social worker and allies wish to utilize a position paper statement are as follows:

> Will the social worker and allies be able to locate a position paper that supports the rationale for the agency policy change?
>
> Will the social worker and allies be able to incorporate the position paper into a persuasive presentation to the immediate target system?
>
> Will a position paper create interest about the agency policy change in the immediate target system?

The second way that a position paper or statement is used by the social worker and allies is by writing and disseminating their own position paper for the purpose of influencing change in an organization. In an article entitled, "Organizational maneuvering: Intra-organizational change tactics" (Cox, Erlich, Rothman & Tropman, 1979), Edward Pawlak relates that social workers often rely on the "case approach" when attempting organizational change. He suggests that a position paper is a "much ignored means of tinkering with organizations." Pawlak defines a position paper as a "statement that sets forth a policy or a perspective. In this instance the position paper (also referred to as a white paper in this article), contains a statement of need and is supported with quantitative and qualitative data. The allies present this type of statement to engender communication and response from the target system. Pawlak (1979) provides an example, as follows:

> A student social worker wrote a position paper identifying the number of teenage pregnancies, the number of associated medical problems, and the high rate of venereal disease among adolescents. She argued for the redirection of the original planned parenthood proposal from the main office to satellite clinics in public housing developments and schools. The paper was well received and spurred the executive to obtain funding from the housing authority.

In this vignette, the position paper was written by the change agent. It not only called attention to a policy situation, it also had the effect of directly influencing the target system (Executive Director and Board of Directors) to secure funding for a policy change. When a position paper is used in this manner, it is employed more as a campaign technique wherein the social worker and allies expect that consensus on the agency policy change will eventually take place.

In the preceding example a position paper was used as a tactic that resulted in the generation of funds to support the agency policy change. The third way that position papers can be employed is related to the writing of funding proposals. In an article by Don Fey (1995) entitled "Prelude to a proposal: the value of position papers," it is stated that position papers draw funding bodies to a cause by setting forth the "organization's stand on an issue, their goals and their recognition of the potential donor's apparent interest in the same issue. The paper may be an informal statement that can be followed by a more formal proposal" (Fey, 1995). Consensus between the agency and funding body is sought and the process is viewed as a collaborative one. Writing a funding proposal is another activity that is important in the Action–Strategy Model and relates to activities that occur in the stabilization process of the change effort. Tips for writing funding proposals are also discussed later in this chapter. Information contained in a position paper could also be included in the introductory section of the funding proposal.

Oral Presentations.   In presenting one's proposed agency policy change, a social worker and the allies will often be called on to make an oral presentation. The coordination of such a presentation should be carefully planned. Content should be adequate but concise and arranged in a coherent manner. Persuasive arguments should be thoughtfully included. Knowledge of the expected audience, and its particular biases, and its current level of information, should be taken into account. One should never assume that the audience already knows and understands current policy, but neither should one "talk down" to a group of decision makers. If needed, include enough explanation and definition to be helpful without being condescending. Avoid use of jargon and "initialese" unless you are positive everyone in the audience is totally familiar with such language. It is also sometimes helpful to include endorsements of your ideas by influential persons. Keep in mind, however, that persons who are influential with you, may not be influential with your expected audience. Oral presentations should be rehearsed using videotaping or voice recorders so that the presenter is familiar with the content, and so that time limits can be carefully adhered to. Always anticipate that there will be questions, try to foresee what they might be, and be prepared with answers. Certain questions that can be anticipated should be incorporated into the presentation.

To summarize, when an oral presentation is required, the social worker and allies should consider the following question and suggestions:

> Will the oral presentation create interest regarding the agency policy change in the immediate target system?

> The social worker and allies should be able to present their ideas about the proposed agency policy change based on the following criteria for presentation content:

>> A clear statement about the overall purpose of the presentation and identification of the policy situation.

>> An overview of client/consumer needs that are unmet, containing facts and statistical data.

>> A concise statement and definition of the proposed agency policy change.

>> A precise statement and definition of the goal of the agency policy change.

>> A clear statement of the objectives that break down the goal of agency policy change.

>> A delineation of the plan of action to accomplish the goal and objectives of the agency policy change.

FIGURE 6.1 Oral Presentation in a Social Work Class

A delineation of the plan of evaluation of the proposed agency policy change that is specific to the goal and objectives.

A brief discussion about the benefits that will accrue to the agency and clients/consumers if the agency policy change is approved.

A summation that highlights the major points contained in the oral presentation.

An invitation to explore alternatives with the immediate target system regarding the proposed change.

The manner in which the presentation is delivered is also important. Verbal communication should be appropriately paced, enunciated, and free of professional jargon. The presenter should be enthusiastic and demonstrate adequate eye contact. It may also be helpful to employ audio-visual aids such as PowerPoint presentations and written documents. Information not readily known by the audience should be supported with citations from scholarly research. Time is of the essence and techniques to encourage questions and feedback from the audience are critical.

Development of Funding Proposals. Another useful tool in preparing for presentation of the proposed change is the development of a funding proposal. In some cases, funding will be sought outside the agency, if the agency policy change is approved. Even when the necessary resources for implementation are available within the agency, the task of developing a funding proposal serves a similar purpose to that of developing a preliminary contract. The process will clarify for the social workers and allies what the necessary resources are, and will prepare them to discuss those needs realistically with decision makers. When funding will be provided from the agency budget, it can be very helpful in convincing decision makers to have a well prepared plan for utilization of resources, especially if contributions from sources outside the agency will defray some of the cost. For example, if the change will result in more referrals from specific agencies whose clients have not had services available, some agencies will be willing to provide transportation for those clients to access the services. Or they may be willing to donate space at their agency for group meetings of those clients if your agency does not have appropriate space available. These would be identified as in-kind services in the funding proposal. If preliminary work on development of a funding proposal has already been done, it may be much easier to convince decision makers that seeking funding outside the agency, when needed, would be feasible. The preliminary work would include a survey or assessment of funding sources that are appropriate and available, as well as the drafting of a preliminary proposal.

For many social workers, the mere suggestion that they might need to write a funding proposal will send shivers of fear their spines. Most social workers look forward to writing proposals just about as much as they look forward to developing policy. It is a task they would much rather leave to the "designated proposal writer for the agency," while they go about the business of "providing services." While it is probably wise that final funding proposals be written by someone with particular expertise in this area (in order to increase likelihood of success), it is still important for all social workers to have a working knowledge of how such proposals are written. It is also important, if they wish to impact or create agency policy change, that they be able to draft a preliminary funding proposal. If their proposed change is approved, and outside funding will be sought, then the person who does such proposal writing for the agency will be able to refine and polish the document.

An understanding of the necessary components of a proposal will be crucial. The monograph, *Program Planning and Proposal Writing* by Norton J. Kiritz (1988) published by the Grantsmanship Center as part of a series on Program Planning and Proposal Writing, identifies the main components of proposal writing.

Summary statement.   Clearly and concisely summarizes the request. While this is the very first section of the proposal itself, it can only be written after completing the other sections. The summary needs to be very carefully written, because it is the first section (and sometimes the only section) that will be read. It must be concise and to the point, but contain enough information to tell the reader what is being proposed.

Proposal introduction.   Describes the agency's qualifications or "credibility." It provides a brief history of the agency and describes its current status. A statement or two from a recent evaluation of the agency, by an accrediting body perhaps, would work well in this section. Remember to keep focused on establishing the agency's credibility and, even more importantly, the reasons why this agency is particularly well suited to receive funding for the specific services being proposed.

Problem statement or needs assessment.   Documents the needs to be met or problems to be solved by the proposed funding. It should answer the following questions:

- Who are the people or agencies with whom the applicant is concerned?
- What is the problem or need on which the agency will focus?
- Is the problem of reasonable dimensions (something that can be changed for the better over the period of the grant)?
- In what direction does the problem statement seem to lead?
- Does this statement appear to be concerned with the needs of clients or with the needs of the applicant?

Program objectives.   Establishes the benefits of the funding in measurable terms or objectives, which then become the criteria for measuring effectiveness of the program, and should tell who will do what, when, how much they will do, and how it will be measured. There must be a differentiation between process objectives and outcome objectives. *Process objectives* refer to the completion of tasks, while *outcome objectives refer* to the benefits of completing tasks. Completion of tasks does not automatically assure that there will be the intended benefit. For example, providing group counseling services, as planned, does not guarantee that the clients who received the services actually benefitted from them. Outcome objectives must be written such that success of the services provided can be measured.

Methods.   Describes the activities to be employed to achieve the desired results. The methods should be understandable, and should be accompanied by an explanation of the rationale underlying your choice of them.

Evaluation.   Presents a plan for determining the degree to which objectives are met and methods are followed. There are two components to the evaluation section. One evaluates the results of your program, or outcome. The other evaluates the conduct of the program, or process. Another way of stating this is that one evaluation considers the question "Did you do what you said you would do?" and the other considers the question "Did that accomplish what you said it would accomplish?" The plan for evaluation must be well developed and well defined. The methods for evaluating and the criteria for determining success must be clearly stated, as well as who will gather necessary data and who will evaluate that data.

Future or other necessary funding.   Describes a plan for continuation beyond the grant period and/or the availability of other resources necessary to implement the grant. Many funding sources are not available beyond a specified time period and will require that you have a plan for continuation of services after that period. This section is where you describe that plan, as well as describe other funding resources—in addition to the grant—that will be utilized to implement the services.

Budget.   Clearly delineates costs to be met by the funding sources and those to be provided by the applicant or other parties. The budget is an estimate of what you believe the costs will be. Included in the budget you present will be the total costs for the various line items, the amount being requested from the funding source, and the amount that will be donated by other sources. The budget format should include two major categories: personnel costs and non-personnel costs. There also needs to be a Budget Summary which, as with the Proposal Summary is written after the budget is finished but is placed at the beginning of the budget section.

Letters of support.   Other useful preliminary work for the social workers and allies, when outside funding is going to be necessary, would be to obtain agreement from other agencies that they will write letters of support for the funding proposal. This indication of support will increase the likelihood of approval by the agency decision makers; it will also be a necessary component of a final funding proposal.

Application of Computer and Electronic Technology.   Encouraging events are currently taking place in social work education in the area of electronic technology. Recent publication of social work texts and workbooks about evaluation of practice, research methods, and statistics, and Internet and computer applications for social work practice are assisting members of the profession to develop assessment tools and improve management information systems (Patterson, 2000; Vernon & Lynch, 2000; Bloom, Fischer, & Orme, 1999; Karger & Levine, 1999; Gibbs & Gambrill, 1998; Karger & Stoesz, 1998; Weinbach & Grinnell, Jr., 1998; Reamer, 1998; Kardas & Milford, 1996; Rubin & Babbie, 1993). In the latest edition of their textbook, *American Social Welfare Policy*, Karger and Stoesz (2002) also discuss areas of concern for social workers related to technology. One such area is the rapidly increasing gap between those having easy access to the use and benefits of technology, and those who do not. This gap is being referred to as the *digital divide*, and has implications for many clients of social workers. Another area that is of concern to social workers is the increased use of the Internet by hate groups, who use this technology to spread their propaganda. In addition to being aware and addressing these concerns, social workers must make use of all tools available to utilize new technology to the benefit of their clients. CSWE recently sponsored a series of national conferences, "Information Technologies for Social Work: Using to Teach—Teaching to Use" as part of the Millennium Project. Presentations about electronic technology and competence are in evidence at annual National Association of Social Workers Annual Conferences including workshops about the Internet, World Wide Web, accessing online systems, and creating agency home pages.

When presenting information to decision makers in the immediate target system, social workers can incorporate electronic technology devices such as Microsoft PowerPoint, scanners, digital cameras, and photo presentations, and agency home pages for publication and client/consumer access on the Internet. The creation of websites for agencies and practice is discussed in a recent publication entitled *Social Work and the Web* (Vernon & Lynch, 2000). Social workers must learn these new skills to remain current and to compete with other human service professions in the twenty-first century. The following questions assist the social worker and allies as they contemplate the usefulness of electronic technology to enhance the plan of agency policy change:

Will the use of electronic technology create interest about the agency policy change in the immediate target system?

Will the use of electronic technology empower clients/consumers to assist with the plan for agency policy change?

Will the social worker and allies be able to incorporate electronic technology based on the following criteria?

- Access current and past "policy situations" including international, national, state, and even local human service agencies that are available on the World Wide Web during the identification and analysis components of the Action–Strategy Model? (Both content and links to social welfare policy are found at sites such as the American Public Welfare Association <www.apwa.org>; Association for Community Organization and Social Administration <www.acosa.org>; Council on Social Work Education <www.cswe.org>; the Electronic Policy Network <www.epn.org>; National Association of Social Workers <www.socialworkers.org>; Policy.com <www.policy.com>; Thomas [Legislative Information on the Net] <www.thomas.loc.gov>; the Urban Institute <www.urban.org>; and, the Welfare Information Network <www.welfareinfo.org>, accessible to the social workers and allies and client/consumers.)
- Access needs assessment and evaluation studies about program effectiveness on the Web?
- Identify and assess target systems through various websites and keyword searches?
- Identify and mobilize the allies by locating appropriate associations, organizations, and think tanks on the Web? (For example, the Association of Baccalaureate Social Work Program Directors has several recommended websites as follows: World Wide Web Resources for Social Workers <www.nyu.edu/socialworkwwwrsw>; Social Work Access Network (SWAN) <www.sc.edu/swan>; Shirley's Social Work Web Resources <www.kml.uindy.edu/resources/socialwork/>; and the Social Work Search.Com <www.socialworksearch.com>.)
- Collaborate effectively with the allies and other interested persons online?
- Use email, listserv/discussion groups, and chat rooms to enhance the flow of ideas and actions regarding the agency policy change?

- Develop agency web pages and/or personal home pages to publish valuable information such as position papers, personal presentations, and funding proposals?
- Elicit feedback and evaluation about these documents by using email links and fill-in forms (Rae and Mellendorf, 1998)?

Model Application to Case Example

In the case example presented in Chapter 3 during the monthly meeting of the agency Board of Directors, both groups attempting change and expansion of an existing policy made excellent use of data that had been collected by staff including survey results about the need for the continuation of the respite home care program and letters of support from key persons in the community. They also distributed draft copies of a funding proposal that had been prepared by group members. It is not mentioned in the case example whether or not the professional staff utilized position paper statements from similar organizations, overhead projectors, or PowerPoint electronic technology, but these techniques would have been appropriate in this type of presentation for the agency Board of Directors.

If Approval Is Obtained, Develop a Final Contract
for Implementation of Agency Policy Change

The social worker and allies have made their presentation to the decision makers and now, finally, have been given approval for the proposed agency policy change. Do they rush out of the room to begin implementation? Of course not! First they need to develop a *final contract* that represents the implementation of the agency policy change. This contract, while it may be very similar to the one they developed as a planning tool, will incorporate any changes or modifications made by the decision makers. The contract may be informal or implicit in nature at this stage. Accountability will be critical to the accomplishment and stabilization of the agency policy change, however, and it will be in the best interests of the allies, the immediate and ultimate target system, to formalize the agreement. It will also include actual beginning dates for activities and realistic time frames for completion. Responsibilities for completion of objectives and tasks may have been altered by the decision makers, and these will need to be reflected in the final contract. Because the *contract* represents an agreement by all persons necessarily involved in the implementation of the policy change, it is important that the contract clearly spell out all activities to be undertaken, and who will do what according to what schedule. To spell out only the major responsibilities, and assume that minor duties will automatically be done, can greatly decrease the chances for success of the change. For example, the best possible plan for a new training program, based on a policy change, can be delayed, if the secretary (or his/her supervisor), was not included in the implementation contract, and the necessary training material was not prepared and copied by crucial dates. Inclusion in the written agreement not only acknowledges that someone has an important role in an agency activity, but their signature increases the likelihood that they have, or will, accept the rationale for the policy change.

As in the preliminary contract, tasks that must be specified in the development of the final contract include the identification and statement of the goal of the agency policy change, and the identification and statement of the objectives. As always, the objectives must be tied to measurement and outcomes. The contract for implementation of the agency policy should also include the necessary steps connected to the evaluation. As with other implementation activities, it should be clearly stated who will conduct the evaluation, what those activities will be (or by what methods evaluation will be done), and by what dates activities will be completed. If the evaluation involves persons outside the agency such as outside experts coming in to evaluate the change, the contract should identify that and the staff member of the agency responsible for securing those persons.

Additional questions about the contract process come into play during this phase, however, as follows:

Identify the goal

Have the social worker and allies reviewed the preliminary contract to determine if it needs to be expanded, or reworded, or discarded?

Have the social worker and allies clearly identified the parties who are agreeing to the terms in the final contract?

Have the social worker and allies identified an alternative goal that needs to be stated in the final contract?

If adjustments are required, is there agreement between the social worker and allies and the immediate target system about the identification of the goal at this point in time?

State the goal

Have the social worker and allies stated the goal that they desire in outcome terms?

Have the social worker and allies identified in the contract who is the ultimate target system, clients/consumers, who will benefit from the agency policy change?

Identify the objectives

Have the social worker and allies thought through exactly what steps are needed in order for the goal to be implemented?

Have they broken down the required activities for implementing the agency policy change into behaviorally specific steps?

Tie the objectives to measurement and outcome

Have the social worker and allies identified the time lines necessary as to when those steps will be carried out?

Have they identified the persons who will be responsible for each task listed?

Have they determined how the effect of the agency policy change will be measured? By what standards and what will constitute success (achievement of the agency policy change)?

Have they included signature lines for every person identified in the contract as having a responsibility?

Model Application to Case Example

In the case example in Chapter 3 during the monthly meeting of the agency Board of Directors, the groups involved in the policy change not only recommended that an existing policy undergo revision and expansion, but also requested that the agency Board of Directors approve the submission of a contract proposal to the Community Mental Health Center. Next, they presented the Board with a draft of the contract that had been designed by members of both groups associated with the change effort. This request was subsequently approved by the agency board with the recommendation that the director work with staff who had been involved in the process to date to forward a final contract to the Community Health Director and the United Way Planning Board for final approval of the funding proposal for the respite home care program.

When the final contract is signed by designated members of the appropriate target systems and the social worker and allies, this action signifies that the plan for agency policy change will take effect. As mentioned in the Preface of the text, the Action–Strategy Model is focused on the development and implementation of a plan of action for convincing decision makers to approve implementation of a proposed change. The four components of the Model, including all of the action steps and selection of a change strategy, focus on the acquisition of skills and knowledge required for social workers to be effective in a very crucial phase of social change: convincing others and gaining necessary approval for agency policy changes that can benefit client/consumers of their services.

Summary

Social workers undertaking an agency policy change usually work in a group with other human service professionals, and must be mindful about group dynamics that can propel or thwart the progress of the change effort. They also recognize that attempting change can be slow and time-consuming, and that their chances of bringing about purposive change are more likely if the change goals remain modest in nature. Courage, persistence, and patience are virtues to cultivate when engaging in incremental change, especially because such change usually does not occur in thirty minutes or an hour. Instead, it may take six months to a year, or even two years, to achieve the desired goal.

It is hoped that the tasks, questions, and suggestions contained in Components I through IV of the Model can be turned into answers that will provide solutions about how you can affect change as a direct service worker. We are optimistic that the discussion about the application of the Action–Strategy Model can assist you to become a macro social work practitioner who is also a direct service worker who possesses the knowledge, skills, and power necessary to bring about change in agency policy.

When social workers intervene to change agency policy that is feasible in nature and extent, they are concerned with how they can use themselves in a meaningful and effective way. They are aware of the behavior, relationships, and ideas of staff and client/consumers in the formal and informal structure of their agency and community. They are also aware of value-laden issues that are generally present in their agency and community pertaining to the policy situation. Further, they are knowledgeable about issues of diversity in the social environment that may impact change and that those issues can affect them as they attempt to influence the immediate and ultimate target systems. Ideas about how values and diversity issues impact the agency policy change process are presented in Chapter 7.

Important Terms and Phrases

Digital divide

Final contract

Position paper and statement

Process and outcome objectives

Learning Exercises

1. Select a human service organization/agency with which you are very familiar. If you are in field placement, you should select your placement agency. Identify a policy that you believe needs to be changed at the agency and then identify both the underlying social issue and the affected client population. If you are not familiar with a local agency, use the following example:

    > A children's residential treatment program, where approximately one half of the residents are there by court order, requires regular participation in counseling sessions by the resident's family, in order for the resident to successfully complete the program. However, due to a scarcity of such treatment programs, many of the court-ordered residents come from distant areas of the state, and more are from low-income families. Participation for these families has been an ongoing problem.

    Next, decide on an organization that would be concerned with the selected issue or population or both. Then, using the material in this chapter on position papers, write a brief (two to three paragraph) position statement, as though you were a group of members of that organization. The position statement should address the larger social issue or the target population or both but should not address the specific policy change for your specific agency. The statement, however, should be written such that it could be quoted to lend credibility to the need for a policy change.

2. Using the following information, write a brief funding proposal that contains all the necessary sections identified in the chapter. Rather than write several paragraphs for each section, it is suggested that you write only a few sentences (just enough to give you a taste of the requirements for each section). An actual funding proposal would, of course, be much more in-depth, and would include a cover letter and attachments. Base your ideas on the following scenario.

> You are a social worker at Agency XYZ. You have been asked to work with a small group of other employees on writing a funding proposal to be sent to a charitable foundation that has as one of its funding priorities the welfare of children.
>
> Agency XYZ wants to submit a proposal for funding to provide special group counseling services to sexually abused children who are in the agency's residential program. The agency statistics show that approximately 40 percent of the residents have been sexually abused. It is expected that a part-time counselor will be needed to direct the special groups and that a psychologist-consultant will need to be available to staff and for emergency situations. The group will need private space to meet and some audio-visual materials, such as films and videos. The agency already has a VCR and a film projector. The only separate room, at this time, is a small conference room that is set up with tables and chairs for staff meetings.
>
> Agency XYZ is a private, nonprofit agency that provides short-term residential care to children, ages ten–eighteen. Short-term generally means ninety days or less.

Annual Statistics:

Provided care to a total of 75 children with the following breakdown:

	Male	*Female*
Ages 10–12	10	13
Ages 13–15	14	15
Ages 16–18	11	12
Totals	35	40

Annual Budget Figures	*Total Budget = $527,840*
Salaries and Wages	341,600
Fringe Benefits	51,240
Facility Maintenance	25,000
Food	50,000
Supplies and Equipment	30,000
Office Supplies	20,000
Miscellaneous	10,000

Current Staff Salaries	
Executive Director	50,000
Administrative Assistant	40,000
Social Worker	30,000
Secretary	20,000
Nurse	25,000

Cook	20,000
Maintenance	20,000
Housekeeper (part-time)	10,000
Youth Care Supervisor (3)	each 25,000
Youth Care Worker	
3 full-time	each 20,000
5 part-time	each 8,320

Study Questions

1. Why do you need to watch for resistance during the implementation of the strategy chosen in Component IV of the Action–Strategy Model? If resistance is noted, what might the social worker and allies need to do?

2. What kind of groups issue position papers?

3. When presenting a proposal for agency policy change to decision makers, how would reference to a position paper be beneficial?

4. What are the key factors in making an effective oral presentation?

5. How is the development of a funding proposal a useful tool in preparing a presentation to convince decision makers to approve a proposed policy change?

6. Are you "computer literate" and knowledgeable about electronic technology that could be helpful in conducting an evaluation or making a presentation about agency policy change? Do you have knowledge of electronic technology and computer applications in various human service organizations in your community? Do you think that human service agencies and social workers lag behind in the field of electronic technology and computer utilization regarding demonstrating the impact of social service programs and social work interventions? Explain.

Values, Interests, and Diversity in Human Service Agencies

Goal Statement

To increase awareness of and sensitivity to values and diversity issues and their impact on policy practice and the delivery of social work services.

Discussion

When social workers have renewed their commitment to social change and have determined to become effective policy practitioners, how do they know what needs to be changed? By whose values do they measure or analyze a given situation? When do they decide to advocate for the values of a minority client group, and when do they focus services to aid in the adjustment of that group to the larger society? Which approach to cultural competence or ethnic sensitivity do they utilize? Which approach is utilized by their employing agency?

The Human Service Agency—"Stirring the Pot"

The pot is the agency and consists of the formal and informal structures. The pot gets stirred in both structures. The formal structure constantly undergoes fine-tuning of its mission, goals, programs, and services from the direct services staff, middle management, and higher administration, the agency Board of Directors, regulatory authorities, and members of the community, for example. Formal organizational activities can be monitored and evaluated through quantitative and qualitative measures and in this sense, it is easier to see what you are dealing with. The informal structure is less easily defined and its boundaries are not restricted to setting goals, objectives, and planning and evaluation processes. Professional and cultural practices and norms present in the agency and the community may exert considerable direction and force having to do with the pursuit of activities, but personalities, gossip, staff perceptions, and conflicts can keep the pot stirred up.

When attempting to bring about an agency policy change, the social worker and the allies need to focus on how people behave in the agency, their relationships to one another, the social structure in which they are organized, and the way that staff perceive, think, and feel about issues. Underlying these characteristics are *values* or "*broad preference patterns* that underlie social behavior, including moral and esthetic components" (Warren, 1977). This means that the social worker must not only know something about the interests and issues of the agency and its staff, the allies, and the immediate and ultimate target systems, he/she must also know something about the values of those groups. So, while it is necessary, it is difficult to ascertain value preferences and priorities of those in a human service organization, as well as those of client groups and the community.

Values Within the Profession

Social work students and social workers can be characterized as "down to earth," low key, unworldly, willing to listen, and ready to discuss concerns with others. They really do not seem to be interested in issues relating to power and money. Many social workers belong to a family that includes a member who is affected by a physical or mental disability. They love to discuss items concerning their personal behavior and emotions. Many social workers hold deep religious beliefs and rely on spirituality and inner strength to help them through the days. They like to talk about values and ethics and think that it is meaningful that the members of the professional organization, the National Association of Social Workers, get together every now and then to revise the Code of Ethics and discuss ethical dilemmas.

It would be an interesting study to discover how many social workers vote for officers of their professional organization at the state and national levels and even more interesting to learn if they know the process about how the Code is revised and what body within NASW is responsible for its revision. It would also be interesting to learn how many social work students and social workers realize that the Code of Ethics contains 155 standards that guide social work practice (Reamer, 1998, 488–500). In our experience, when the question is asked about how social workers incorporate the values and Code of Ethics in their practice, usually the answer is: "I don't think about consciously integrating them as I conduct myself according to those values and ethics in everyday life. They just make sense to me."

Many social work students and social workers seem to be unaware that there is a national education accrediting body known as the Council on Social Work Education that is responsible for setting standards for social work curricula at the graduate and undergraduate program levels. Social work educators, however, are acutely aware of the Council on Social Work Education educational policies and guidelines for accreditation, especially around the renewal of accreditation time period. Social work faculty constantly present information about social work values, and the Code of Ethics throughout their curricula. They think that social work students and social workers enter a human service agency environment either in their field placement settings or their first jobs armed with a professional value base and a Code of Ethics. In addition to wanting to "help people," it is hoped that students and workers manifest an intense interest in and concern about gender differences, minority groups, people of color and human diversity, and that they want to tackle issues that impact social injustice and discrimination of disadvantaged groups.

David Gil (1998) raises questions about whether "social work practice has been consistent with the mandate of its Code of Ethics to pursue social justice and resist oppression." He answers himself by remarking that it seems to be "that although social workers and their organizations tend to abhor injustice and oppression, they usually do not challenge their systemic sources in capitalistic dynamics." Moreover, in actual practice, in spite of their values and ethics, social workers are typically not involved in efforts to confront and transcend injustice and oppression and their roots in the fabric of society. They tend to consider their practice as politically neutral, and they separate it, therefore, from their philosophical rejection of injustice and oppression. In reality, social work practice is ultimately connected to social welfare policy. As one student in a social welfare policy class remarked, "I had no idea that social work practice was so political!"

Values and the Relationship to Change

Whether analyzing or implementing existing policy, or developing a new policy, social work practitioners are operationalizing values. This is often done without realizing either what values are being served or what those values are. The values may be clearly reflected in the stated policy (*explicit*), or they may be unstated, or *implicit*. Policy may be serving both explicit and implicit values simultaneously. As practitioners, social workers frequently do not recognize or acknowledge the implicit values in a given policy, even though they can verbalize the explicit ones. However, in order to effectively impact existing policy, create needed changes, and develop new policy, it is necessary for social workers to become more deliberately aware of the values underlying their policy practice.

What then are values, and how do they impact on policy practice? In the book *Social Work Macro Practice*, *values* are referred to as "strongly held beliefs" (Netting et al., 1998). In their text, *Introduction to Social Work and Social Welfare*, Macht and Ashford (1991) define values as "our beliefs about people, human nature, and what we see as good." *Values* are defined by Robert L. Barker (1995) in *The Social Work Dictionary* as "customs, standards of conduct, and principles considered desirable by a culture, a group of people, or an individual." These beliefs or values exist on many levels, which include personal values, community values, and societal values. In addition, there are values belonging to specific groups such as ethnic or cultural values, religious values, and values of professional groups and labor organizations, as well as identifiable occupational groups such as farmers and artists. Values of groups of people are referred to as *ideologies*, and those ideologies, or value systems will shape the political and economic structure of the group and of society, as well as influence our personal value systems (Macht & Ashford, 1991).

Social work is a profession based on values and it takes a hopeful or positive attitude toward people; in fact, we might see it as a *"profession of hope."* The values of respect for all people and the right to self determination imply that people can change. Now, while many professionals believe that people "can" change, social workers believe that people "will" change, given sufficient opportunity and necessary assistance. In other words, social workers believe that what they do makes a difference. They are, therefore, always hopeful. Lest you think this is a "pie in the sky" kind of belief, let us assure you that any social worker who has practiced for very long is well aware that not every client wants to change and not every situation can be altered sufficiently to facilitate their change. But overall, most social workers remain hopeful, in spite of those challenges. Such an attitude toward clients and the environment in which they live makes social workers natural *change agents* or those who are desirous of bringing about changes. It is the sincere belief of the authors that social workers can and must expand their focus of change in clients and their environment to include change in human service agency policies. The same hopeful attitude that sustains social workers in direct service work will enable them to address the growing need for awareness of their involvement in policy practice.

In policy practice, social workers are considering policy situations and issues, always aware of the possible need for change. They make choices about what needs to be changed as well as the means for accomplishing that change. "The choices workers make about the ways to approach the change process stem from their underlying theory of human behavior and reflect their values" (Miley, O'Melia, & DuBois, 1998). Also impacting on those choices will be the value systems of the various groups involved in the change situation—clients/consumers, agency or organization, community, and funding sources.

Assumptions and Constraints

The social worker, contemplating the undertaking of a change process in agencies or in social environments, needs to make some assumptions before engaging in the change process. Such necessary assumptions include that there will be resistance or *constraints* to the change effort, as well as support and *affirmation* of the effort. These constraints and affirmative activities will be found in both the formal and informal structure of an organization. Social workers also need to assume that change is ongoing, and any change effort they may engage in will be an effort to direct the existing change in a particular way. They also must assume that any particular change they may attempt will have desirable and *undesirable consequences*, that is, results that they did not intend to occur. They must be willing to assess the possible undesirable consequences in order to answer the question: "Is it worth it?" That question must be asked before beginning any change effort and at each step thereafter. Either a yes or no answer may be a valid response to that question, depending on a careful analysis of both costs and benefits of the possible change effort. Another assumption that must be made by the practitioner considering change is the fact that values or moral standards may be in conflict in any given social situation. Therefore, the social worker may be required to choose between legitimate values in order to attempt to effect change.

Having agreed that constraints will exist, what might they be and where might they be located? One constraint may be a difference in interpretation of the given situation, which is often linked to differing values among the persons involved. Many people in this society believe it is best to leave something alone unless an obvious problem exists, "if it isn't broken, don't fix it." Some people, on the other hand, see situations and look for ways to enhance or improve them. Social workers, as part of their training, are taught to see situations in this latter way, and to work from a strengths perspective, while much of the society feels that a response is appropriate only when there is an obvious problem. Even when everyone involved has agreed that a response is appropriate, a difference in interpretation, based on values and cultural norms, may cause disagreement over what part of the situation requires changing. For instance, one person may believe that a policy change needs to occur to enhance services that would increase independence and individuality in a group of clients, while another may feel that policy needs to enhance services that increase group cohesiveness and emphasize the "common good." While both are obviously valued by people in this society, operationalizing one in a given situation may decrease or obviate the other.

Another constraint that may exist in a given situation is the cost of responding or *costs of change*. It would be a mistake for a social worker to analyze a situation and assess that there are no costs involved. When one includes as costs the time and energy required to initiate a change effort and then, if successful, to implement the change, there is always a cost involved, even when additional funding is not required. Administrators and other decision makers will consider these costs as well as the other funding requirements, and a wise social worker acting as a change agent will also. In addition to the fact that changing habits, or how we do things, requires an expenditure of energy, the social worker seeking change must assess and understand any values attached to doing things the existing way. The more important any attached values may be, the more energy will be required to change how things are done.

Other constraints may include personal values that interfere with an individual's willingness to join a change effort. Such legitimate values as not creating dissension, avoidance of conflict, and yes, even supporting one's family, can all become constraints in developing support for a given change. Every person involved in a change effort needs to weigh the relative importance of the values attached to changing a situation with the risks involved. Unfortunately, there is no set formula for doing this. While it is a professional obligation of every social worker to do everything possible to improve the life situation of clients, each social worker must consider how much personal risk is legitimate for him/her in any given situation.

The social worker must also become aware of how personal values may be impeding their ability to accurately assess a situation or their planning for appropriate response. Personal values are not always recognized as such and may even be misunderstood to be professional or societal values. An example of this occurred in a recent discussion among students in a Field Practice Seminar, led by one of the authors. The discussion was focused on *value conflict* situations and methods of resolution. A student shared that he/she was having a value conflict situation in their placement agency, an agency that served adolescents with behavior problems in school. In a particular case situation, a young male student had been initially assessed as having social skill deficits, and the student intern was asked to carry out a plan to increase social skills. Every other time the intern met with the student the plan was to engage in conversation, or whatever the student and intern agreed was most helpful. The alternate meetings with the student were to involve playing basketball, most likely with the goal to increase the student's confidence in sports activities and thereby make him more comfortable interacting with peers. The social work intern shared with the group that this plan made him very uncomfortable. He did not see how the student's preference for isolating himself and reading instead of engaging in sports activities was a problem. He also noted that in making several observations of the student in the classroom, he had observed the student interacting appropriately with some peers who were more like himself. The intern identified that his professional value of client self-determination made him uncomfortable with requiring the student to spend part of his time playing basketball when he obviously did not enjoy doing so.

A lively discussion followed this sharing, centering around the value of client self-determination, and the social work intern's experience of conflict around this value, even questioning whether the agency was violating that professional value. Apart from suggestions that the intern needed to share his recent classroom observations with the social worker who developed the treatment plan, and what his professional obligations were to the placement agency, the discussion had not surfaced any questioning of the intern's stated value conflict being at a professional level. Having remained rather silent throughout the conversation, another social work student suddenly asked: "Would you feel as strongly about client self-determination if the student wanted to do the reverse. If he wanted to always play basketball and neglected required reading, would you still think client self-determination should take precedence?" The student who raised the issue, as well as most of the others, was suddenly very quiet for a few seconds, and the discussion then shifted to the need for recognition of one's personal values and how they may be infiltrating situations without our awareness. As the social work student shared with this author in a later conversation, "When he asked that question, it blew my mind."

Understanding values, then, is a necessary prerequisite of engaging in a change effort. Particular values, or morality, are often considered to be connected to some universal truth by those who hold them. However, even when people agree on a particular set of values, they may still have different *value preferences or priorities*. In other words, they seldom agree on the relative importance or priority listing of those values. The practitioner must realize that not all values can be maximized or operationalized simultaneously, but value choices must be made, even when there is agreement on the individual values involved in a given situation (Warren, 1977). For example, all staff in an agency may agree on the value of a client's right to self-determination, as well as the value of protection of children. They may have varying opinions, however, on which of those values should take precedence in developing family counseling programs and deciding whether participation in those programs should be limited to voluntary clients or should include involuntary or court-ordered clients.

When values are of relatively equal importance it is inevitable that conflict will arise between those values. In an article by Tropman (1995), which looks at value conflicts as experienced by policy planners, he states that "the most difficult policy choices involve making a decision . . . between two or more good choices or two or more unsatisfactory choices." He goes on to explain that not only does society have important values that are in conflict with one another but that those values can be best understood by being organized in opposing sets of value dilemmas. Tropman identifies seven such sets: individual/family; self-reliance/interdependency; secular/religious; equity/adequacy; struggle/entitlement; private/public; and, work/leisure (Tropman, Erlich, & Rothman, 1995).

Value Dilemmas	
1. individual/family	suggests the need to balance between our own needs and the needs of our family.
2. self-reliance/ interdependency	emphasizes the strain between the desire to "go it alone" and the need to depend on others.
3. secular/religious	suggests the tension between looking for rational explanations for life's ups and downs and turning to religious sources for support.
4. equity/adequacy	refers to the conflict between fairness to all and the responsibility to help those most in need.
5. struggle/entitlement	suggests the tension between the importance of working for everything we get and being entitled to certain things just because we are human beings.
6. private/public	describes the conflict between use of personal or corporate means, the use of government to achieve desired social goals.
7. work/leisure	confronts the issue of work and its meanings. How much work should we do, and for how long? When should work stop and leisure begin?

FIGURE 7.1

From *Tactics and Techniques of Community Intervention* (p. 69), by John E. Tropman, John L. Erlich, and Jack Rothman (Eds.), 1995. Copyright 1995 by F.E. Peacock Publishers. Reprinted with permission.

Interestingly enough, the values on the lefthand side of the pairs, as pointed out by Tropman, are the dominant values of our society. The values on the righthand side of the pairs are subdominant in society, but they are the values emphasized by the profession of social work. Thus, as we go about the business of operationalizing our professional values in our work, we will inevitably be in conflict with the values of the larger society. And, to the extent that we are successful in our work, we will be altering and shaping new dominant values for society.

Another value question for the policy practitioner is, "How to know what people's values are?" How might we decide what is best for a group of people? The only way to know for sure would be to arrive at consensus, and this would be unrealistic in many situations, so practitioners often have to settle for methods that provide the best possible assessment of what is important to the group in question. Such methods include polls, surveys, and use of representative democratic systems.

Values and the Agency Policy Change Process

Goals

Values are linked to each component of the agency policy change process. To begin with, the selection of the goal of a change effort has value implications. The first value question to be addressed is, "Should we try to change the existing situation?" Another question involves the process of determining the goal—what process is best? Due to personal and societal values, most social workers would be inclined to favor a democratic process for selecting the goal. However, that is most likely to require modification of the goal. Then the question arises about how far one is willing to go in compromising his/her original idea before he/she is unwilling to continue in the change effort. Another value question having to do with the goal is to determine how great a change to attempt to accomplish. While many times one can see the benefit of a goal that represents major change, the chances of success are less. A useful fact to keep in mind is that the greater the change, the greater the resistance is likely to be. Based on this fact, *solution-based incrementalism* seems more practical and likely to succeed. Even though small change is more likely to support the existing system, unless one is attempting a radical change, such as restructuring the system, incrementalism is generally a more practical approach. The value question for the practitioner, then, becomes one of finding the degree of change that represents the best balance between the values attached to the need for change and the values attached to success.

Allies

The next value question in the agency policy change process is the identification and mobilization of the change allies. Should we require that the allies have the same values as we do, or just that their values about the change effort are similar to ours? Given that the values of each individual participant in a change effort are likely to be different, or, if they are all similar, that value priorities are likely to be different, it is unlikely that a practitioner attempting change will be able to limit the allies to those just like himself/herself. The question then becomes one of how much difference one can accept. If a person who wishes to assist in accomplishing change has values that are not only different, but are in conflict with those of the change agent and other allies, should that person be incorporated into the change system? While that question cannot be answered without considering each particular situation, it is helpful to again recall the saying, "Politics makes strange bedfellows." So can any change effort! Sometimes even those with very different values can be very useful in accomplishing change, such as the radical outspoken person that is rarely agreed with who, by his/her extreme comments, forces everyone involved in a change effort to carefully think through their own beliefs and opinions. This is a question that must be considered very carefully by the social worker attempting to engage in a change effort.

Another question to be considered is what kind of change system will be used in the change effort. Generally speaking, when considering system types from the most open to the most closed, the values of social workers would favor a more open kind of working system. However, the more open system requires more sharing of power and decision making, which results in greater likelihood of the change goals being modified. The value conflict for the practitioner then becomes one between values attached to the goal and the value of democratic processes. According to Roland Warren (1977), there are three kinds of system structures possible in a change effort, as follows:

1. highly controlled with change goal set by a few, and the means to reach the goal set by a few
2. change goal set by a few, but the means to reach the goal set by many
3. very open with the change goal and the means set through a participatory process involving many.

The question that must be asked by the social worker attempting change is, "How wide can the participation process be without seriously altering the goal?" Or another way to ask the question is, "Whose change goal will be sought?" It is interesting to note that there is a tendency for change efforts to move in the direction of a more closed system, even when beginning as an open system (Warren, 1977). Over time, task and decision-making responsibilities become delegated to smaller groups in the interests of efficiency so that total participation no longer exists. The larger the group of people engaged in a change effort, the more likely this is to be true.

The Change Target

Value questions that pertain to the choice of target are generally connected to the ultimate (client/consumer) target. There is a tendency to focus on deviant behavior and to see client/consumer or client groups as the target for change, rather than to identify the factors that impact on clients as the necessary focus for change. This is referred to as *blaming the victim* (Ryan, 1976). While we recognize that changes in behavior on the part of clients are often necessary and desirable, it is very tempting to allocate the majority of energy and resources to this end, and leave little for addressing the need for system changes. For example, there are conflicting studies showing varying levels of success with the Workfare concept aimed at poor, female-headed households to prepare them for employment in the secondary labor market. As social workers we can agree or disagree with the concept, but we can all agree that most of the attention in welfare reform in the past ten years has been focused on changing behavior of welfare clients.

Selection of Change Strategies

Given a choice between using *change strategies* of cooperation/collaboration, campaign, or contest, most social workers would quickly choose cooperation/collaboration because of its strong personal and societal value. However, even when cooperation/collaboration is a possible choice, there is a question of the value of cooperation and accord compared to the value of tackling a controversial issue, but one that has significant benefit to clients. Conversely, in choosing cooperation/collaboration, there is a value question regarding the social worker's willingness to cooperate with the existing power structure in order to obtain the change goal. This issue is particularly problematic if the power structure itself is seen as needing change. The level of discomfort a social worker experiences with disagreement can influence his/her ability to perceive when a situation is not appropriate for a cooperative strategy. The level of discomfort may be increased or decreased by a worker's belief regarding the possibility of multiple truths in any given situation.

Campaign, as a strategy choice, also contains value issues. When a social worker has selected the change goal and, through campaign tactics, attempts to persuade others to agree with that objective, there is always the value question of one person deciding what is best for others. While the social worker acting as change agent may in fact have crucial knowledge and may be better able to identify the best change goal, this does present conflict with the social work ethic of self-determination. Another possible value problem with the use of campaign strategy is that the tactics utilized often "look like" educational tactics. Information is presented in a persuasive manner, but where education generally presents all sides of an issue, persuasive efforts generally present only those arguments likely to convince. This has value implications for the practitioner. One only has to watch an infomercial on television to understand the difference between a campaign effort and true education. If, however, the value of the change goal is significant, the change agent must compare that to the value of discussing and presenting all sides of the issue in his/her effort to convince decision makers to make changes.

The third strategy choice consists of contest strategies. A major value conflict exists around the question of using these strategies at all. Because contest strategies contain an element of coercion, one wonders if they are ever justifiable. The value conflict is generally based on our strong value of cooperation and our hesitance to engage in anything that has conflict or coercion inherent within. However, in a situation where the value of the change goal is so high, to do nothing is unacceptable, and where other strategies could not succeed, a contest strategy may be the only value alternative. Given that contest strategies include either attempts to convince a third party, and thereby defeat opponents, or attempts to eliminate the opposition (as in recall or impeachment efforts), the change agent certainly can see the necessity and value of these strategies.

The final value question regarding the choice of strategies is that of *congruence between means and end*. Another way of understanding this is to consider the level of agreement between methods used and the purpose of the goal. For the practitioner, this is sometimes a question of considerable complexity. Regardless of the high moral value of the goal of the change effort, there can be value conflict around the methods used to reach that goal. Many believe that means and end cannot be separated and that there must be congruence between them. For example, if the goal is to increase cooperation between administration and line staff by establishing an advisory council of consumers and staff representatives, and the existing power structure is adamantly opposed, does the social worker as a change agent employ contest strategies and attempt to get the key members of the existing board recalled? There is no clear answer to this question that can be nicely applied to every case scenario. Value questions must be struggled with as they arise by the persons involved in the situation, and they will be determined by the relative strength of the values involved.

Having clarified for ourselves the value issues involved in the policy change situation and in every component of the change process, can the issue of values be considered resolved? The answer of course is no. Value conflicts can arise again at any time and are seldom resolved once and for all. In addition, diversity issues need to be considered. While they are being discussed separately, values and diversity are integrally connected. How one responds to diversity issues will be determined by one's values, and values of diverse groups are likely to contain significant differences, which can affect any given policy situation.

Diversity Issues—Two Approaches in Human Service Agencies

Diversity issues are equally important to value issues for the policy practitioner who wishes to accomplish policy change. At every step of the process, from identifying a policy issue that needs changing through the implementation, stabilization, and evaluation of the change, the practitioner must consider both the values as well as any diversity issues involved. Most social workers consider themselves to be sensitive to most diversity issues, and yet many social workers have blind spots of insensitivity, of which they are generally unaware. Diversity issues cover a very wide range of issues, including but certainly not limited to race, ethnicity and culture, religion, gender, sexual orientation, disability, and medical conditions. There are two approaches commonly used to address diversity issues in the human service arena, and both contain value questions. Many agencies and human service organizations utilize both approaches; some use one or the other.

The first approach is described by some writers as the *ethnic[ally]-sensitive* approach in that there is a conscious effort to provide services to ethnically and racially diverse populations through hiring of persons from those ethnic and racial groups. The underlying premise seems to be that those client groups will receive services more effectively when services are provided by those similar to themselves. In his article in the journal *Administration in Social Work*, Burton Gummer (1998) discusses this idea in relation to achieving diversity in the workplace. He states that "Most people assume that workplace diversity is about increasing racial, national, gender or class representation." He goes on to say that people attempt to do this by either encouraging women and people of color to blend in or by setting them apart in jobs that relate specifically to their backgrounds. He believes that this is based on the assumption that the main benefit in having identity groups in the organization is the knowledge they bring of their own people. He also believes that this is both limiting and detrimental to diversity efforts. He suggests that the major benefit of having a diverse workplace is that "they bring different, important, and competitively relevant knowledge and perspectives about how to actually *do work*."

It is important to note that many writers do not define ethnic-sensitive practice with this limitation; in fact, many include the provision of services by "outsiders" within the definition. In their book *Ethnic-sensitive Social Work Practice*, Devore and Schlesinger describe ethnic-sensitive practice as paying "simultaneous attention to individual and systemic concerns as they emerge out of client need and professional assessment" (1999). They go on to discuss seven layers of understanding that represent the professional perspective and explain how these seven components may need to be viewed expansively in order to attain ethnic-sensitive practice. Iglehart and Becerra (1995) describe ethnic social services as "those provided by members of ethnic groups for members of the group."

A practitioner who wishes to be *ethnic-sensitive* would need to become aware of these ethnic agencies and their policies and services. In spite of definitions that include provision of services to diverse populations by practitioners outside the particular group, there is still a conception among some organizations that to deliver ethnically sensitive services, the services must be delivered by ethnically similar workers. Students need to understand that both opinions exist and are adhered to "in the field."

The second approach is more recent and is one where a conscious effort is made to increase and enhance the sensitivity to diversity of all staff. Here the underlying premise is that everyone can effectively provide services to diverse groups if they are sensitive enough. This approach is embodied in what NASW refers to as *cultural competence*. In the revised Code of Ethics, it is stated that social workers should understand culture (and more specifically the culture of their clients/consumers) and its function in human behavior and society. It is further stated that they should recognize the strengths that exist in all cultures. They should be able to provide services competently and sensitively to those cultures (NASW, 1996 and 1999). What does it mean to be competent? One definition of competence is the capacity to perform a specific task (Linzer, 1999).

Another example of professional efforts to operationalize cultural competence, which is focused on a specific client population, can be found in an article in the journal, *Social Work*, entitled "Cultural competence for transracial adoptive parents." In that article, Elizabeth Vonk emphasizes the importance of knowledge, attitudes, and skills and goes on to say, "It is not enough to be aware of how race and culture affect self-functioning; individuals also must be open to learning about the effect of race and culture on others, to learning about racism and mechanisms of oppression, and to acquiring the cross-cultural skills that enable effective intervention" (Vonk, 2001).

In a discussion of cultural competence, then, we obviously are referring to a practitioner's capacity to effectively deliver services to specific populations whose cultures are diverse. It is not enough to be open-minded and friendly. Competence requires the acquisition of knowledge and skills. In considering the issue of competence, it may be useful to note the tests of capacity sometimes used to ascertain the cognitive ability of certain clients to participate in decision making (or their competence). Those five capacity areas to be assessed are (1) being able to indicate a choice, (2) having factual understanding, (3) having ability to reason rationally, (4) having an appreciation of the nature of the situation, and (5) having reliable outcomes of choice (McKinnon, Coumos, & Stanley, 1989). If we generalize from these capacity areas and apply them to a social worker who is required to deliver services to a client or clients who are culturally, ethnically, or racially different than the worker, it becomes clear that an open mind and a willingness, while necessary, are not enough to be competent.

In her book, *Breaking the Ice: A Guide to Understanding People from Other Cultures*, Daisy Kabagarama (1993) states that,

> developing an appreciation of other cultures is a difficult process given the fact that our past has been rooted in divisions based on race, class, religion, gender, ethnicity, residence and age. We need to look at the world from a perspective that does not equate difference with inferiority. Such an approach sees human beings the world over as striving to make meaning out of life and adapt to their environments. It is a result of a conscious effort to understand and respect fellow human beings irrespective of whether they are like us or different from us. It also calls for empathy toward those whose conditions are less desirable than our own.

Expanding the Diversity Discussion

Up to this point, our discussion of diversity has focused on ethnic and cultural sensitivity/competence, and is intended to include racial and religious diversity as well. However, this discussion has not focused on other diversity issues, such as gender, age, sexual orientation, and all the other differences included in a definition of diversity. Perhaps we need to expand our thinking about culture so as to include all the other diverse groups. Or perhaps a new term is needed that requires social workers to be diversity sensitive, or *diversity competent*, so that it becomes more apparent to a practitioner who is delivering services to two female partners raising children together, for example, that there is a need for the practitioner to be sensitive to diversity issues that may be involved, and to be competent in delivering services to those specific clients.

The *Code of Ethics* of the National Association of Social Workers refers to sensitivity to *social diversity* (1996). In addition, the NASW Board of Directors approved Standards for Cultural Competence in Social Work Practice on June 23, 2001. This document delineates ten standards for social work practice related to cultural competence. The introduction to those standards acknowledges that the term "cultural diversity" has been associated with race and ethnicity, but is now expanding to include other diversity experiences. The introduction concludes by stating that "cultural competence in social work practice implies a heightened consciousness of how clients experience their uniqueness and deal with their differences and similarities within a larger social context." The standards themselves, without the introduction and interpretation material, are as follows:

Standard 1. **Ethics and Values**—Social workers shall function in accordance with the values, ethics, and standards of the profession, recognizing how personal and professional values may conflict with or accommodate the needs of diverse clients.

Standard 2. **Self-Awareness**—Social workers shall seek to develop an understanding of their own personal, cultural values and beliefs as one way of appreciating the importance of multicultural identities in the lives of people.

Standard 3. **Cross-Cultural Knowledge**—Social workers shall have and continue to develop specialized knowledge and understanding about the history, traditions, values, family systems, and artistic expressions of major client groups that they serve.

Standard 4. **Cross-Cultural Skills**—Social workers shall use appropriate methodological approaches, skills, and techniques that reflect the workers' understanding of the role of culture in the helping process.

Standard 5. **Service Delivery**—Social workers shall be knowledgeable about and skillful in the use of services available in the community and broader society and be able to make appropriate referrals for their diverse clients.

Standard 6. **Empowerment and Advocacy**—Social workers shall be aware of the effect of social policies and programs on diverse client populations, advocating for and with clients whenever appropriate.

Standard 7. **Diverse Workforce**—Social workers shall support and advocate for recruitment, admissions and hiring, and retention efforts in social work programs and agencies to ensure diversity within the profession.

Standard 8. **Professional Education**—Social workers shall advocate for and participate in educational and training programs that help advance cultural competence within the profession.

Standard 9. **Language Diversity**—Social workers shall seek to provide or advocate for the provision of information, referrals, and services in the language appropriate to the client, which may include the use of interpreters.

Standard 10. **Cross-Cultural Leadership**—Social workers shall be able to communicate information about diverse client groups to other professionals.

How then, does one become diversity competent? Certainly the beginning point is to genuinely agree with the value of diversity and to adhere to the ethics of the profession which say that we should be culturally or diversity competent. Having made that commitment, it is necessary for the social worker to acquire knowledge about diverse groups, and to take advantage of every opportunity to develop skills based on that knowledge. Is there a clear-cut, simple, step-by-step curriculum, which will automatically make a practitioner culturally or diversity competent upon completion? Of course not. It has been our experience, just in addressing the task of reviewing current material on this subject, that there are as many opinions on the definitions of and solutions to the issues of diversity, as there are writers on the subject. The personal struggle to organize thoughts and to present current thinking in a focused manner is the struggle we all must be willing to engage in if we genuinely want to become competent in delivering services to diverse groups. We often become so nervous about learning and understanding the specific information about one group that we lose focus on the broader aspects of diversity issues. On the other hand, we are concerned that as we broaden our focus and incorporate all diversity into our thinking, we may inadvertently dilute the importance of each group's struggle for respect and fairness. For example, as we consider current material on cultural competence and recognize that it is focused on racial and ethnic groups, we wish to see other diverse groups included in these conversations. However, we are worried that to include a discussion of the culture of the elderly and the importance of sensitivity to their needs, we may lose the intensity of the discussion of cultural norms of Hispanic families, or Native American communities.

Becoming culturally or diversity competent is an ongoing process that must continue throughout one's professional life, and to engage in that process will require a willingness to struggle with the complex issues involved in serving diverse people. A neat, tidy definition or a simple step-by-step process is not likely to engage the practitioner in the soul searching necessary to develop genuine sensitivity to those who are different from themselves. Neither can practitioners immerse themselves in another's culture or lifestyle and magically arrive at "sensitivity." To be sensitive to another first requires an acceptance and understanding of one's own group membership. Even if the practitioner is a member of a group normally thought of as "diverse," there is no automatic sensitivity to all others dissimilar to oneself. Social workers can, however, through their own ethical and professional training, give respect to all people, regardless of group membership. But to be sensitive to the needs of others whose needs may grow out of experience and group membership very unlike our own and whose needs may, therefore, be very different from ours, requires much more than respecting others. It requires changes in attitudes and it requires skill development based on a willingness to acquire knowledge on an ongoing basis, and to be always learning about diversity issues.

Kabagarama (1993) argues that "social change occurs when people change the way they perceive some elements constituting their world," and "that change can be spurred by a charismatic leader, a dramatic event, or a gradual awakening through education."

Diversity and Values: Connections and Conflicts

How are diversity and value issues connected? While it may seem obvious to state that each cultural group has its own values, it is worth noting that values may differ from one group to another, and even when the values of groups are similar, they may be prioritized differently. In considering change, the practitioner must also consider the possible value conflicts connected to culture. Assessment of the change situation, development of policy, implementation and evaluation of the policy all can be affected by misunderstanding the values involved. While there may be a common value of work between two cultures, in some cultures responsibility to family takes priority over the value of work. That could affect how a social worker interprets data on absenteeism in a work training program, or even how the program gets developed and implemented. It is important to remember the concept from Roland Warren's work that even when values are shared, they are not always prioritized similarly and that all values cannot be operationalized simultaneously (1977).

Another example of value conflicts connected to culture would be the task of implementing licensing regulations for foster homes when there is a need to recruit specific cultural groups for licensure. Licensing regulations are generally based on the values of the larger society, and can present conflicts for particular cultural groups within that society. For example, there is a common rule that does not allow children over a particular age to sleep in the parental bedroom, unless medical or mental health reasons require this practice for an individual child. This rule is based on the value of the larger society to develop independence and also on the "need for privacy" for adults. In particular cultures, the development of independence is not so highly valued, and some have developed the practice of having children sleep in the parental bedroom as the norm. In fact, while it may have developed as a practical solution to living situations, such as living space and warmth, this practice is connected to the value of the family as a unit, as opposed to the value of individuality of each member. In dealing with this situation, the practitioner needs to understand the values involved, both the culture of the family and that of the larger society.

In responding, the practitioner has some choices, each requiring cultural sensitivity. He/she can interpret the norms of the larger society in a manner that is respectful and sensitive to the culture of the family involved, leaving the choice with the family to adapt or to decline licensure. Or the practitioner can request a waiver of the particular rule for this particular family, using the official process for such requests. Again, sensitivity to both cultural values would be required. Another option for the practitioner would be to begin the process of getting the rule changed, so that the rule itself reflects exceptions for certain situations. All of these options involve change at some level, and all require practitioners to be aware of and sensitive to diversity and value issues. Is it an option for the practitioner to simply respond by saying, "You don't meet the requirements of the rule. Sorry, no license."? Yes, that is an option, but it may not be a viable one in many situations. As our society is becoming more and more diverse, incorporation of diversity values must be faced. While as a profession we see this as a "good thing," the operationalizing of this is likely to be complex and difficult, and will be made up of hundreds of situations similar to the one described. To simply attempt to respond to each one by imposing existing values from the "majority" culture would be resistant to the changes that are occurring around us. As policy practitioners, we must be willing to consider the need for agency policy change as never before.

Summary

As acknowledged at a recent NASW Annual Leadership Meeting, "a mixture of races and ethnic backgrounds will dominate twenty-first century culture, and social workers must be on the front lines of a drive for multi-cultural awareness" (Hu-DeHart, 1999). This increase in diversity will be accompanied by changing values within our society. It is imperative that social workers be sensitive to both diversity issues and their accompanying values. Any successful effort to accomplish policy change in human service organizations or communities will require a careful analysis of the values and value priorities that are attached to the situation as it is (the status quo) and those that would be impacted by a change effort. Failure to do so will result either in unsuccessful attempts to change agency policy or in policy that does not provide effective service delivery.

Important Terms and Phrases _____

Affirmation
Blaming the victim
Change agent
Change strategies
Congruence between means and end
Constraints
Costs of change
Cultural competence
Diversity competence
Diversity issues
Ethnic sensitivity

Explicit values
Ideologies
Implicit values
Profession of hope
Social diversity
Solution-based incrementalism
Undesirable consequences
Value conflicts
Value preferences/priorities
Values

Learning Exercises_____

1. Choose a group of people you think have similar values: the members of your immediate family, group of members of your church, or a group of social work students. Do a survey of the values of those people by asking each person to identify ten of their values. Record their responses. After each person identifies his/her values, then ask him/her to prioritize them with number one being the highest priority. Compare the values of the group members, noting the number of values that are identified by several members of the group. Also note the differences in priority for those values that are identified by more than one group member.

2. All cultures and most people claim to place a high value on *family*. Prepare to discuss this with someone by, first, preparing an interview instrument. Be careful to include questions that explore their values/beliefs about family, but also explore how they operationalize that value. For example, you might include questions that describe a situation involving a conflict between work and family, and ask them how they would respond to the situation. Try to think of some other ways to discover how the value is operationalized. Also be careful to use some open-ended questions and be sure that the questions themselves are not culturally biased.

3. Find a person from a group who is culturally different from your own, and who is willing to discuss his/her values with you. Interview that person using the instrument developed in the previous exercise. Use the results of your interview to engage in a discussion of variance between and within cultures, in a group setting, such as your classroom.

Study Questions _____

1. Choose a well-known public policy such as work requirements for female-headed families receiving public assistance. Identify some explicit values that are being served by the policy.

2. For the same policy, identify some implicit values that may be served.

3. What are some of the constraints that will exist in any change effort?

4. What is the significance of value preferences or value priorities in understanding value conflicts?

5. How are values connected to choice of strategies?

6. Identify the differences between the ethnic sensitivity and the cultural competence approaches to diversity issues.

8

Agency Policy Change, the Practice of Social Welfare Policy, and Social Work in the Twenty-First Century

Goal Statement

To present ideas about how social workers can use the Action–Strategy Model to bring about policy change in larger systems and why they need to possess knowledge about transformations in political and economic environments at the federal, state, and community levels.

Discussion

> *It is questionable whether the profession of social work has as much impact regarding major institutional change today as it did in the old days of fighting for minimum wages, tenement house laws, child labor laws, and the rest* (Warren, 1973).

Are Professor Warren's remarks as insightful today as when he wrote them in 1973? Will social workers in the twenty-first century contribute as significantly to societal well-being as did their predecessors of the early and mid-twentieth century? We believe that direct service social workers, middle-level managers, and agency administrators can come together in their own agencies and link with others in the community to bring about change. Sometimes agency policy change is based on activities that occur in larger societal systems such as the creation of laws and new regulations in state and federal governments. Sometimes, however, the reverse can also be true—an agency policy change at the local level can create a rippling effect that extends to state and congressional levels of decision making.

A case example is presented in this chapter that describes a change at the state governmental level that involved adult foster care licensing rules and regulations. The seeds of change were initially sown at a community agency by social workers and human service professionals who were concerned about living conditions of residents in adult foster care facilities. The Action–Strategy Model is discussed in light of these changes that were brought about by social workers within their local agency and then expanded at the state level.

Dream About Change Beyond Your Local Agency and Community—Regional, State, and Federal Systems Levels

Social workers do indeed have the right to intervene in the lives of clients/consumers. This right often flows from public policy and laws that enable and fund social welfare programs and human services. Like it or not, the creation, implementation, maintenance, and elimination (if unjust and discriminatory) of government policy at the federal, state, and local levels is necessary for the future of the practice of social work regardless of the appropriation and allocation devices and whether or not programs and services are delivered by public, nonprofit, or for-profit organizations that exist at those same levels.

Privatization and *purchase of service* agreements (whereby government contracts with agencies at all levels to plan for and deliver human services) are the preferred funding arrangements at the present time. They may fall from favor, however, depending on the political winds, economic conditions, societal expectations, and, more importantly, performance evaluations of their effectiveness in getting vital services to those consumers who are supposed to benefit from social welfare policies. Social workers, by virtue of their Code of Ethics, are supposed to engage in *policy practice*. These activities are "those professional efforts to influence the development, enactment, implementation, modification, or assessment of social policies, primarily to ensure social justice, and equal access to basic social goods" (Barker, 1999). This basically means that we need to exercise our influence at the federal, state, regional, county, city, township, and school board levels. The question is how do we do this in an effective manner?

While it is the responsibility of all social workers to initiate change in agency policy in their respective organizations, the profession still appears to be relying on traditional *office model practice* approaches. Gone are the days when we can sit in our offices and engage in fifty-minute clinical sessions, dictate or scribble a few notes regarding the interview, and move on to another client/consumer unless, of course, we want to be out of a job within the next two months or less! The savvy practitioner of the twenty-first century also interacts with professional staff in other human service organizations, develops educational presentations regarding programs in their own agencies, conducts needs assessments, seeks out new funding sources for innovative programs to serve diverse constituencies, and constructs electronic web pages to market information about their agencies and programs for publication on the Internet (Vernon & Lynch, 2000).

Just as the great civil rights leader, Martin Luther King, remarked, "I have a dream," social work students and practitioners can also dream about how life can become better for oppressed populations and those who are treated unjustly. The question becomes, however, "Can social workers turn their dreams into change goals?" The answer is a resounding "yes." A case example that demonstrates how social workers can apply the Action–Strategy Model beyond their own agencies in larger political arenas is now presented.

A Case Example

The Local Level.   Direct services workers of a local public welfare organization, including two CSWE professionally educated social workers, were unhappy with the lack of specificity of licensing ordinances and regulations for adult foster care and group homes for elderly, mentally ill, and disabled persons. The rules were initiated and administered by the city housing authority. Many homes were poorly staffed and operated by persons with little background or training for caring for persons with special needs. Client/consumer needs in those homes often were not met or ignored, and there was little that could be done by social workers to remedy the plight of the residents because the existing licensing ordinance was broadly written and lacked detail about safety mechanisms and protection of the residents. Staff at the public welfare agency had no jurisdiction over the local housing authority and the ordinance had been in existence for a number of years. Formal and informal communication channels between the two organizations about the ordinance had deteriorated.

Several advocacy groups had attempted to call public attention to the existing conditions but were unsuccessful in their efforts. The public welfare workers knew that the rules regulating these types of homes were of little or no benefit to clients/consumers. They also knew that many residents were suffering from lack of proper care, inadequate sanitation, and minimal safeguards. Something had to change. To test the hypothesis that practically anyone could apply and receive a license for an adult foster care home and that any type of building structure where residents were placed could be approved, one social worker at the public welfare department applied to the local housing authority for a license. The address listed on the application was a garage that was owned by the worker, located near the worker's house. Approximately three weeks later, the social worker received approval from the housing authority that certified the garage as an acceptable adult foster care home. After recovering from the shock of receiving the license, the worker proceeded to show it to co-workers and two supervisors in the organization. Eventually, a group composed of two social workers, three professional staff workers, and two supervisors requested a meeting with the director of the agency in order to make known the bizarre course of events involving the licensing of a garage as a suitable placement for adult foster residents.

Initially, the director of the agency was appropriately dumbfounded, but as ideas were discussed about possible remedies to deal with the situation, the director advised caution on the part of the professional staff, but stated that the three Board of Director members of the community public welfare organization should be notified. One of the members of the Board, who was a retired social worker, a respected citizen of the community from a well-established family, and an advocate in county and state political circles for persons with mental illnesses and disabilities, requested and received an appointment (also agreed to by the other Board members) with the editor of the local newspaper to discuss the ordinance. The editor thought that the situation deserved investigation and decided to send a photographer and reporter to the garage for pictures and a news story. The story was published complete with photos and a summary of the weaknesses of the existing licensing ordinance. State legislators, city council members, and county commissioners responded and expressed embarrassment and outrage. Eventually, the local licensing ordinance was rescinded and a tentative agreement was reached between the local housing authority and the public welfare agency that included new provisions for the adult foster care homes. A contract was drawn by the city attorney and approved by the city council. This document set forth stricter eligibility rules for licensing of the homes and improved physical and safety regulations for residents. The contract became the foundation for the operating policies and procedures regarding adult foster care in the community for staff in the local public welfare organization and housing authority.

The State Level.　　Due to the publicity about the conditions of adult foster care homes in this particular community, state legislators, lobbyists, and advocacy groups had become involved. After the ordinance change had taken place in this community, it was eventually replaced three-years later by state-wide rules that set forth improved safety and protection regulations for persons placed in adult foster care homes. During that three-year period, professional staff of the local public welfare agency, including the social worker who originally applied for and received the license for the garage, worked with several advocacy groups, state legislators, staff in the state public welfare department, fire marshals, representatives of veteran's organizations, nursing home lobbyists, and prosecuting attorneys to advise, draft, and lobby for reform. The direct service workers and their supervisors provided testimony at public hearings, offered technical assistance to members of various state-wide organizations, and became members of an advisory committee at the state and local levels. After the state law was passed by the legislature, those same workers implemented and administered the improved licensing law. The workers also assisted home owners to comply with the new law. As mentioned, the time frame for this change was three years, beginning with the printing of the initial newspaper story in the community, and ending with the passage and implementation of a new state law.

Application of the Model to the Case Example

The Model, while uniquely suited to incremental agency policy change, contains the basic components necessary for bringing about change at the regional, state, and federal levels. The preceding example illustrates how social workers can dream about agency policy change to improve the lives of their clients/consumers, and how the change, when implemented, can extend to larger systems, such as a state legislature. Although the Model is theoretical in nature, it is helpful to examine how its major components could be used to guide workers throughout the change process, as presented in the case example.

I. Dream About Agency Policy Change.   Perhaps the social worker and agency colleagues dreamed about ways that clients/consumers of adult foster care homes could benefit from well-regulated facilities. The worker who applied for the license for the garage may have been shocked into reality when it was approved. Whatever the reason, at this stage of the process, the worker's imagination conjured up something better than "business as usual" regarding the quality of life for adult foster care residents. Nevertheless, the deliberate choice to submit the application for licensing eventually brought the worker closer to achieving the goal of safety and protection for residents, not only at the local agency level, but state-wide as well.

II. Analyze the Policy Situation Related to the Change Idea.   In this example, the underlying question for the direct service workers became: "Is it possible to improve the quality of care, safety, and protection for residents of adult foster care homes in this community?" They were beginning an intervention in an already existing situation. They were directing their attention to how they could change the course of events in a policy situation to make it more responsive to client/consumer needs. The existing policy was contained in an ordinance of the local housing authority which was responsible for the investigation, administration, and implementation of the rules governing adult foster care facilities. Workers in the public welfare organization coordinated placements in those homes for mentally ill, disabled, and elderly persons. The agency policy they followed as found in their operations manual addressed itself to arranging effective placements and maintaining a supportive environment for residents of these facilities. This policy assumed that foster care homes were suitable for clients/consumers. Despite the fact that the local housing authority was responsible for the enforcement of the ordinance, public welfare workers and clients/consumers of their services were impacted by the lack of its specificity and meager enforcement.

The change idea became one of improving the physical and social environment of local adult local foster care homes. Some of the particular ideas that the workers talked about were securing more staff to supervise residents, safer building structures, and prompt investigations of applications for licensing. The direct service workers were aware of the fact that their own organization was a bureaucracy governed by state and federal laws and policies. They discussed their change idea among themselves, but realized that they would need to talk with their supervisors, and those persons, in turn, would discuss the situation with other agency supervisors and eventually with the director of the organization, and, finally, with members of the board of directors of the local public welfare department. Because the chain of command must generally be followed in a bureaucratic organization, the workers, supervisors, and agency director realized the consequences of not following the rules of communication and recognizing various roles and status positions of all involved. By the time that the discussion reached the board of directors' level, the situation had changed. It would have been unsuitable for agency staff, including the director, to discuss the situation with the editor of the local newspaper. Although risky, it was, however, quite legitimate for a member of the board of directors, who also happened to have a state-wide reputation of being a long-time advocate for the mentally ill, to present the matter to the editor of the local newspaper as one that merited attention by the community.

At this stage in the development of the policy situation, a working hypothesis about the policy situation was formulated in the minds of the workers, supervisors, and agency director when the member of the Board of Directors presented the policy situation to the newspaper editor and an article was published. The working hypothesis was: *Our idea will result in the improvement of the physical and social environment of adult foster care homes in our community.* Improvement eventually did come about as a result of the initial activities of the "allies" who initially dreamed and acted to bring about change. The news story and community outrage about the lax rules for adult foster care homes also led the housing authority staff to improve the ordinance and its enforcement. No one involved in the local effort was counting on the immense interest generated state-wide by this policy situation, however. As with many activities related to social welfare policy creation, initiation and implementation, there are always unanticipated consequences attached. Those who were involved at the community level had not conceived of the change extending to a larger system— the state legislature in this example.

III. Develop a Plan of Action Related to the Change Idea.   The original allies in this example were the social workers, direct service workers, and their supervisors. They were joined by the public welfare agency director and later by a member of the board of directors of the local welfare agency. While differences existed among the allies, they were in agreement that something needed to be done about the condition of community adult foster care homes. A formal determination of need was not undertaken by the allies in this situation, although the newspaper editor and reporter conducted a survey of existing community adult foster care homes and gathered research about the application, investigation and monitoring procedures carried out by the housing authority. Their findings revealed that applications were "rubber stamped" for the most part and that there was little monitoring and investigative activity except when a crisis occurred involving abuse or neglect of a resident. The newspaper staff also examined adult foster care licensing on a state-wide basis and published this information in follow-up editions. It was subsequently learned that the situation in the local community was consistent with what was happening throughout the state.

With the advent of this information, the policy situation evolved from one with a local identity to a state-wide issue replete with ramifications for numerous municipalities and public welfare organizations. As is typically the case and as there is movement to larger systems, it is likely that increasingly larger forces come into play to produce change. Another corollary also appears that as support is sought from others in the change process, the initial group of allies begins to lose some degree of power and control over the process. The larger force that eventually came into play was the state legislature, which passed a state-wide licensing law for adult foster care homes. The enforcement of the new law removed the local housing authorities from regulating the facilities and placed the rules in a special unit within the state public welfare bureaucracy.

The direct service workers, supervisors, agency director, and member of the Board of Directors (the allies) identified the immediate or initial target system as the local housing authority and the ultimate or long-range target system as the residents in the adult foster care homes. The allies were united. The ultimate target system composed of the residents was fairly powerless although their relatives and family members were involved and interested in the course of events. As the scenario unfolded, the composition of the allies changed to include legislators, state-level bureaucrats from public welfare, housing, mental health, and aging services; representatives of state-wide associations of nurses, social workers, trial lawyers, and fire marshals; advocates of the mentally ill and aging; members of the League of Women Voters; residents of adult foster care homes and their families, *and* the social workers, direct service workers, their supervisors, the agency director, members of the Board of Directors, and the newspaper editor. The immediate target system also changed from the local housing authority to the state legislature and its social services legislative committee in the House of Representatives, which voted the bill out of that committee and recommended its passage by the legislature as a whole.

Change Strategies—"Mixing and Phasing"

The direct service workers, supervisors, and agency director employed a collaborative strategy in the early stages of development of the policy situation. All who were involved were in total agreement that action was needed to improve the local ordinance. The member of the Board of Directors adopted a campaign strategy with the newspaper editor, who, in turn, used a combination of campaign (persuasion) and contest (social action) strategies through newspaper articles with the idea of inducing change at the local level. When the local ordinance governing the licensing of adult foster care homes was rescinded and rewritten, the strategy employed by staff of the public welfare agency was also one of campaign as a degree of persuasion had to be used to convince the staff of the housing authority to agree to needed changes in the ordinance.

Once the momentum was extended to the state level, collaborative strategies such as task-oriented planning, state-wide needs assessments, and surveys of community enforcement ordinances and consensus planning were used by policy analysts employed by legislators and state bureaucracies. Campaign strategies appeared in the repertoire of advocacy groups. These included testimonials at regional public hearings from adult foster care residents and family members, lobbying efforts by social workers and nurses, and letters to newspaper editors throughout the state. The original allies, or those who initiated the change at the local level, remained involved by attending public hearings and working with state policy analysts on the drafting of the legislative rules after the bill had become a law. As there was a high level of interest and the issue was valued by a broad constituency concerning the creation of a state-wide law regulating the licensing of adult foster care homes, conflict strategy was not used in this change effort at the state level. There was some discussion about possible demonstrations by adult foster care residents and their families on the lawn of the state capital grounds as a mechanism for calling attention to their needs, however. In this example, there was a mixture of change strategies employed by various persons at different times. Tropman and Erlich refer to this process as the "*mixing and phasing of strategies*" wherein the "practitioner moves from one strategy to another as shifts occur in the conditions affecting his[/her] overall objectives" (Cox et al., 1987).

Development of a Preliminary Contract

A form of a tacit preliminary contract at the local level took place when the news article and community outrage forced the housing authority to take action. Goals and objectives were not spelled out at this stage, although a formal contract phase between the city housing authority and the public welfare agency was begun. Informal evaluation was undertaken by the professional staff and members of the Board of Directors of the public welfare organization, and the newspaper staff who followed the story. Informational meetings between the two organizations took place and were attended and reported in the newspaper. During these meetings, ideas were discussed about specific items that were to be included in the new ordinance. Barriers between staff from the housing authority and public welfare workers dissolved as verbal exchanges between these two groups took place. These exchanges laid the groundwork for the formal construction of the new ordinance.

At the state-wide level, a bill was introduced by a coalition of Democratic and Republican legislators. This is the best of all possible worlds because it implied collaboration between all parties involved. A collaborative and cooperative environment is the most desirable, even more so when partisan politics are in operation. A bill can be thought of as a preliminary contract. Once the bill was assigned to the social services legislative committee, the monitoring and evaluation of the process was automatically begun and regulated by legislative protocol regarding time limitations and reporting requirements. The Committee gathered testimony from public hearings, policy analyses of staff of state bureaucracies, and testimony of social services staff, social workers, and adult foster care home residents. The bill was unanimously voted out of the Committee process. At this juncture, the bill had been amended and carried with it a series of recommendations that could also be considered a preliminary contract for implementing a new licensing law for adult foster care homes. These recommendations formed the foundation for the drafting of the final bill.

Opposition and resistance to the bill was evident in public hearings held during the Committee deliberations. The state-wide association of adult foster care home owners protested passage because compliance with the requirements contained in the proposed law would result in expensive financial outlays for their members with existing foster care homes. Eventually, the adult foster care home owners group was successful in securing wording in a section of the law that established a state-wide advisory committee to be housed in the state public welfare department. The purpose of this committee was to assist with the drafting of the administrative regulations of the licensing law. Members of the home owners association were assured that a proportion of the advisory committee membership would be drawn from their membership. The formation of an advisory committee was successful in allaying some of the concerns voiced by the home owners regarding the passage of the law although it did not totally *eliminate* their resistance to the proposed new rules.

Implement Change Strategy for Approval
of Agency Policy Change

At the local level, the housing authority initially resisted the policy change as it meant that there would be more responsibility and additional work for staff to enforce stricter rules and regulations. The change strategy that brought about immediate reaction was one of contention when the newspaper editor published the article about the marginal condition of those who resided in adult foster care homes. While the initial reaction of the housing authority and the city council was one of shock and denial, when the fires cooled and factual data were introduced, the change strategy that worked for the allies in this example was one of campaign. The allies had to consistently use persuasive approaches such as the presentation of documents regarding the physical and mental functioning of the residents and their opportunities for activities within the homes to enhance their social and mental capacities, literature reviews about successful adult foster care homes in other sections of the country, and staff training programs for the employees in various foster care home settings. This strategy, coupled with the newspaper publicity and input from advocacy groups, eventually wore down the resistance of the staff of the housing authority and an ordinance was finally drafted by the staff of the city attorney's office and voted by the City Council. After its passage, the directors and key staff members of the public welfare and housing authority organizations engaged in a mutual exchange of ideas about how the new ordinance could be administered for the benefit of clients/consumers. Proposals were written by the direct service workers and their supervisors and presented to the housing authority staff by the director of the public welfare agencies. Counter-proposals and amendments were discussed. The staff of the city attorney's office subsequently constructed a formal contract containing the responsibilities of the housing authority staff and the supporting roles that would be taken by the public welfare organization staff workers and supervisors.

Three years later, an adult foster care licensing bill was unanimously passed by both branches of the state legislature and signed into law by the governor. The law, in essence, represented the final contract that set a state-wide agency policy change in motion. It also made the state public welfare department responsible for the administration, implementation, and evaluation of law. The advisory committee was established. It included representatives from a wide range of groups with ties to adult foster care, including representatives of the adult foster care home owners association. The advisory group was convened by the director of the state public welfare organization and was charged with the responsibility of writing specific rules and regulations that would govern all adult foster care home licensing. The group met on a bi-monthly basis for one year in order to review and finalize rules, which were then assessed by the state legislative services bureau for legality. The new rules and regulations were subsequently published in paperback version and distributed to interested persons and groups throughout the state.

Social workers and direct services workers in a community agency dreamt about a better quality of life for their clients/consumers in adult foster care homes.

They made a commitment to change something rather than to complain and do nothing. They became serious, told their supervisors, and were inspired by them and their agency director in creating interest in the issue through a local news story. They felt good about themselves when the city council passed an ordinance to improve the existing one, thus guaranteeing more safeguards to the residents of the homes. They felt at ease when they coordinated placements in adult foster care homes for their clients/consumers. They were amazed that their actions led to the passage of a state-wide licensing law. They were honored that their opinions and input were valued by legislators and policy analysts. They were pleased when a member of their group was asked to serve on the state-wide advisory committee to write specific rules and regulations. They were excited when the licensing rules were finally published because they could rely on a state statute that provided legal back up for their interventions when protecting residents in adult foster care homes.

Ten Principles to Consider When Social Workers Attempt Policy Change at All Intervention Levels

Social Welfare Policy Is the "Beginning," Not the "End," of Social Work Practice.
Jansson (1999) differentiates between the terms "policy practice" and "policy advocacy." *Policy practice* is defined as activities to "change policies in legislative, agency, and community settings, whether by establishing new policies, improving existing ones, or defeating the policy initiatives of other people," while *policy advocacy* is a form of intervention designed "to help relatively powerless groups," as distinguished by color, gender, ethnic background, age, and mental and/or physical disability. Policy practice and policy advocacy are often combined as social workers provide service and interact with those who are in need of service or are discriminated against. These activities may take place in a local agency or through the provision of testimony to a legislative committee. Wherever that action takes place, social workers need to be present to fight against social injustice and assist their clients/consumers to secure access to effective services.

In the twenty-first century social work practice with individuals, families, and groups continues to be affected by social welfare policy decisions at all governmental levels that are characterized by legislative actions, judicial decisions, and administrative rules and regulations administered by staff in bureaucracies and human service organizations.

If social workers desire to meet the basic human needs of people, they must understand that the creation or expansion of social welfare policy, a subset of public policy, constitutes the "beginning" point of activity—not merely the ending phase that is far removed from their interventions at the agency level. Social welfare policy dictates what is possible at the agency level. Social workers cannot practice without it.

Social Work Services Are for Everybody.   Social work, by virtue of its history, mission, and value base, is uniquely suited to focus on the alleviation of conditions that affect poor persons, people of color, and diverse populations that are oppressed and discriminated against. Advanced generalist and generalist social workers of the twenty-first century are also equipped and prepared to serve persons from all economic and social groups whose lives are in jeopardy and who find themselves dealing with catastrophic events such as severe illness, trauma, or disaster. Policies that allow us to apply our generalist skills and knowledge must be in place in local agencies as well as set forth in state and federal laws. If social workers desire to work with people from all walks of life, then we must advocate for the institutionalization of our profession and the delivery of human services in America and internationally, as well.

Social Workers' Knowledge of Social Welfare Policy Empowers Workers and Clients/Consumers.   The basic reason that social work students and workers study social welfare policy is to convey their knowledge about various laws, programs, and services to clients/consumers to educate and enable them to make decisions that will benefit their quality of life. The idea is that this process transfers decision-making power from the professional to the consumer. Empowerment is a popular concept, but how can social workers empower clients/consumers when their own basic knowledge and grasp of how social welfare policy works is meager and lacking in basic understanding about the governmental process? Social workers must improve their basic knowledge about how government works *in addition* to improving their practice skills with individuals and families.

Knowledge of States Rights and Federalism Is Important for Social Work Practice. Social work students and workers must become aware of the role played by the concept of *federalism*—the particular relationship of the federal government to its constituents, the states. The Founding Fathers of the American Revolution were distrustful of a strong, central government, yet social welfare policy and the profession of social work in America witnessed its greatest growth and expansion during a period when the federal government was steadily increasing in centralization and power—from 1932 during the administration of Franklin D. Roosevelt to 1980. During the Reagan administration, which began in 1980, the profession began to witness a deliberate dismantling of the welfare state and devolution of federal policy to the states and local units of government. The thinking goes that liberals, with whom social workers have been heavily identified during the past century, favor a strong central government to protect the rights of those who cannot protect themselves. The conservatives, with whom social workers have not been heavily identified, espouse the rights of states and local government regarding decisions about the need for and creation of social welfare programs via the block grant process. Social workers are still reeling from the block grant process and devolution of social welfare policies emphasized during the last two decades of the twentieth century, instead of poking their noses into areas where new funding mechanisms are popping up at the local, state, and federal levels. This is a sad state of affairs given the precedent of Harry Hopkins, Frances Perkins, and Wilbur Cohen, who stuck not only their noses but their minds and beliefs into the creation of major social welfare policies such as the Social Security Act, the Fair Labor Standards Law during the 1930s, and Medicare during the 1960s. Today, the decision-making pendulum has swung to state and local units of government and away from the federal government. Collaborative community efforts are vital in these days of privatization, managed care, and local control. If social workers desire to work with all people, they must improve their basic knowledge of the political shifts that take place between federal, state, and local governments.

Government Belongs on the Backs of Social Workers

I always thought that government was dumb and stupid, and I had no interest in learning anything at all about it. Now that I have learned how dependent human service organizations are on it, I think that I had better pay attention to it. —Student in an introductory social welfare policy course, Fall 1998.

Harold W. Demone, Jr. in his analysis of how the United States population viewed government at the end of the twentieth century, offers these conclusions:

1. government is too large, and should be substantially decreased in size;
2. taxes should be reduced;
3. governmental functions should be transferred to governments closer to the people;
4. a safety net should be retained for the worthy poor, but not as an entitlement;
5. the unworthy poor are to be on their own (Gibelman & Demone, 1998).

Regardless of whether students and social workers agree with the preceding statements, it is unlikely that government at the local, state, and federal levels will go away and that human service organizations will be able to function without the help of some form of governmental assistance such as grants or direct allocations from federal and state bureaucracies. As discussed by Dolgoff, Feldstein, and Skolnik (1997), "government is not the enemy some see." They suggest that, "The ultimate questions should not revolve around the issue of whether or not government should intervene but, instead, should be focused on when, where, and how governmental interventions will be most helpful for the individual and society."

It behooves social workers and students to educate themselves about public policy and government organizations if they wish to survive in the twenty-first century. Government continues to influence the social welfare environment, so how can social workers use the resources offered by government programs for clients/consumers in their own communities? Another question must be answered before agency and community social workers are able to address the first question and that is, "What do social work students understand about the connection between government, social welfare policy, and social work practice at the agency level?" If students and workers are unable to make the connection, the alternatives for the profession are bleak indeed.

Social Workers Are Political Scientists.   This text does not focus on the history of social work and social welfare policy, its analysis, and formulation. It is not a political

science text that provides the student with basic information about the purpose and function of government. There are numerous texts that contain this information such as *Social policy and welfare: A Clear Guide* by Burden (1998); *American Social Welfare Policy: A Pluralist Approach* by Karger and Stoesz (2002); *Communication, Citizenship, and Social Policy: Rethinking the Limits of the Welfare State* by Calabrese and Burgelman (1999); and *Social Policy and Social Programs: A Method for the Practical Public Policy Analyst* by Chambers (2000). Social work students and workers need to read or re-read these texts to understand exactly who, what, where, when, and why they can apply pressure to decision makers on behalf of the consumers of human service organizations. Also, re-read the U.S. Constitution, especially Article I, Section 8: "To lay and collect taxes. . . to pay debts and provide for the common defense and *general welfare* of the United States" as discussed in *The Court and the Constitution* by Cox (1987), and in other books such as *A History of American Law* by Friedman (1991); *We hold these truths: Understanding the Ideas and Ideals of the Constitution* by Adler (1987); and *The Great Rights of Mankind: A History of the American Bill of Rights* by Schwartz (1977). These readings will shed light on the question of whether or not the inclusion of the phrase "general welfare" in the U.S. Constitution provides justification for the creation of social welfare laws at the federal level.

Another area of political science is the body of knowledge about political elections, partisan politics, and working in coalitions with other professional disciplines to affect change in societal systems. Social workers need to know about how candidates are elected to office and the manner in which Democratic, Republican, and Reform Party activities influence the making of social welfare policy. There are numerous texts, monographs, and pamphlets published about these topics such as *Affecting Change: Social Workers in the Political Arena* by Haynes and Michelson (2000); *Becoming an Effective Policy Advocate* by Jansson (1999); *The Policy-based Profession: An Introduction to Social Welfare Policy for Social Workers* by Popple and Leighninger (1998).

Social workers must re-educate themselves about the political process.   The political climate of "reinventing government" espoused by the Clinton-Gore team that was adopted early in that presidential administration, meant that the lines between public, nonprofit, and for-profit organizations were blurred regarding the delivery of "governmental" functions. Actually, those lines had been blurring since the days of the American Revolution, but in the twenty-first century world of social welfare, it is increasingly difficult to determine whose responsibility it is to provide health, safety, protection, as well as educational human services such as child welfare to clients/consumers. These services are provided by public, nonprofit, and for-profit corporations and organizations that co-exist in any given community in America. *Privatization* refers to "the government transferring one or more of its functions to the private sector as a gift, for a nominal sum or for the full value of the operation" (Gibelman & Demone, Jr., 1998). As federal and state governments appropriate and allocate funds for those operations, privatization, purchase-of-services agreements, and managed care will continue to be highly politicized in our society. As these approaches generate controversy and contradictory opinions in political circles, and given the fact that today they dominate and dictate service delivery, the practice of social work and human services at the agency level will also continue to be highly politicized, controversial, and contradictory. Public, nonprofit, and for-profit human service agencies depend on local, state, and federal funds for their existence. It therefore behooves social workers to educate themselves about the political process at all of these levels. Policy changes that social workers initiate and implement at the agency level can have an impact at the state and federal levels as well.

Social workers are agents of political change.   The political activities of social workers are summarized in an article by Wolk, Pray, and Weismiller (1996). The authors state that social workers continue to keep abreast of political decision making that affects the poor and oppressed members of society and that they are as politically active when compared with other professional groups. The authors also note, however, that beyond voting and keeping informed, social workers are less likely to engage in political activities such as lobbying, campaigning, and offering testimony. Also of interest in the article is information to the effect that social workers employed in macro-social welfare organizations such as those found at the state and federal levels are more likely to engage in visible political activity than their direct service counterparts found in local community agencies.

The purpose of the above-mentioned article was to encourage social work educators to include field practice settings of a political nature such as a state legislature or congressional setting at the BSW and MSW educational levels—simply to generate more interest in the policymaking process as critical to the future of the profession! It appears that social work students are not heeding this "call to arms," however, given the current fascination and romance with counseling individuals and families, despite the constraints placed on their practice by privatization and managed care regulations. *Managed care* has impacted the time that workers actually spend with clients and consumers. Social workers also grapple with value-laden and ethical considerations connected with managed-care practice. Becoming active in political campaigns, making financial contributions to candidates, testifying before legislative committees, and running for public office are areas where social workers can also make a contribution, regardless of which partisan affiliation they may identify. This type of participation means that social workers act to change or reform managed care approaches, for example, rather than merely reacting to rules and regulations passed by members of a legislative body far removed from the day-to-day activities of "helping people." Social workers do not need to become politicians but they must become agents of political change in order to affect the social services delivery system.

Social Workers Are Economists.   This text does not concentrate on concepts regarding economic ideologies that influence the creation of social welfare policy. There are many books, monographs, and journal articles that address the importance of these ideologies and their impact on the making of social welfare policy, such as

Essays on the Welfare State (Titmuss, 1963); *Regulating the Poor; the Function of Public Welfare* (Piven & Cloward, 1971); *Assets and the Poor: A New American Welfare Policy* (Sherraden, 1991); and, *Growth, Redistribution, and Welfare: Toward Social Investment* (Midgley, 1999).

Social work students and workers must recognize, however, that values and ideological beliefs about how social welfare programs should be funded, who should be eligible for services, and how long benefits should be extended, are reflected in the behaviors of elected officials who appropriate those funds. The values and ideologies of decision makers who exercise great power and control in the policy area are characterized by controversy and contradiction. For example, the passage of the Social Security Act, the major showpiece of social welfare policy in America, is currently under discussion concerning future funding devices, fiscal considerations, benefit levels, and eligibility for benefits. The Social Security Act was controversial when it was introduced and passed by Congress during the mid-1930s, yet the effect of its passage has greatly reduced poverty among the elderly, especially during the latter part of the twentieth century (Karger & Stoesz, 1998).

The Social Security Administration redistributes taxes in the form of social security benefits to those persons who qualify. Just about everyone age sixty-five and older is eligible for some type of benefit from this policy, and the numbers of those persons who will become eligible in the twenty-first century continue to place heavy demands on the solvency of the system. Social welfare programs that redistribute income and that characterized the American social welfare state during several decades of the twentieth century, are coming under closer scrutiny as evidenced in current economic development proposals and approaches. Critics of the redistribution function of social welfare programs—cash and in-kind benefit programs to fund health and social welfare services for those persons living in poverty or slightly above the poverty level such as Social Security benefit and Supplemental Security Income grants—claim that these programs drain the economy of resources as income is consumed by the beneficiaries as opposed to directing economic resources into production and investment channels. If social workers want to continue to work with people, then we must become knowledgeable about social welfare programs such as Social Security, Medicare, and Medicaid, which will continue to be closely examined. It is no longer safe to assume that these programs will be around in their present form in the twenty-first century due to the enormous expenditures and outlays of capital required for their continued existence. Social workers will want to be at the discussion table, as they were during the Roosevelt, Kennedy, and Johnson presidential administrations, so that they can present fresh, new alternatives and ideas for social policies and programs to benefit those clients/consumers who are in need of assistance and service.

Social Workers Build Strengths and Assets in Clients/Consumers.   Asset building in clients, consumers, and communities, the strengths perspective in social work practice, and the development of social programs that contribute to economic growth in a positive fashion, all relate to the production aspect of the economic cycle rather than the consumption side that is associated with draining the economy of needed investments and income. Given the growth in population, longer life expectancy, dwindling resources, and fewer employed workers to support older persons at the national and international levels, it is obvious that social welfare and social workers need to design new approaches to deal with meeting human needs. It behooves the profession to study and understand political and economic ideologies that impact social welfare policy regardless of whether these reflect liberal or conservative perspectives.

Agency Policy Change Is Compatible with the Values and Ethics of the Profession of Social Work.   It is possible to apply the four components of the Action–Strategy Model to social welfare policy change at the regional, state, and federal levels, if social workers keep an open mind and are objective about the political process and are guided by the Code of Ethics. Just as the social worker engages a client/consumer in a joint and objective decision-making process to achieve a goal, it is paramount that the worker keep in mind that policy change activity is just that—a process that is jointly shared and objective in nature. Politics evokes highly charged values and interests about controversial and contradictory issues on the part of those involved in the process of decision making. How many times do social workers become overly involved with their clients/consumers? Or grow angry, or frustrated, or upset, or impatient? However, politicians are not clients/consumers of therapeutic interventions, so the skills and knowledge needed to work with them and their staff must relate to their political behavior, not therapy and helping with personal concerns.

Just as direct service practitioners, administrators, and middle management link with others in their own agencies to promote agency policy change, and staff in various community organizations collaborate on program development to deliver quality services to clients, they develop an understanding about the need for policy development at the broader and larger systems of social change. Agency policy is a microcosm of the larger regional, state, and national policies. There is an interdependence between local agency policy and state and federal policy. The social welfare world of today is very different than that same world in previous decades of the twentieth century. Privatization, contracting, purchase of service agreements, and managed care are the inputs and through-puts of the majority of social service delivery systems with increased emphasis on outputs that reflect collaboration between agencies, comprehensiveness of community services, and outcomes associated with cost reduction and effectiveness, and accountability regarding client benefits (Gibelman & Demone, Jr., 1998). All of this does not mean that social workers cannot carry out the values and ethics of the profession. In fact, to act otherwise may result in an abandonment of those principles.

The World Is Not Perfect.   It is the job of social workers to call attention to imperfections in political, economic, and social systems just as our great role model, Jane Addams, did more than a century ago. Her accomplishments in the fields of child welfare, juvenile justice, and the peace movement are well known, and she was a "key architect of what might be called the grass roots welfare state. And she had no rival, then or now, in giving voice to the egalitarian ideal that has stimulated what is best in the American reform tradition" (Kazin, 1999). A direct quotation from the book, *A Useful Woman: The Early Life of Jane Addams* (Diliberto, 2000), as cited by Kazin, is relevant for social workers to embrace, as follows: "The blessing which we associate with a life of refinement and cultivation, must be made universal if they are to be permanent. . . . The good we secure for ourselves is precarious and uncertain, is floating in midair, until it is secured for all of us and incorporated into our common life." It is an imperfect world. While social workers attempt to remedy injustice, eliminate discrimination, and wipe out poverty, efforts directed to these ends are on-going in the twenty-first century. The idea is that we continue to work in an effective, consistent, and solution-based manner to do just that.

Summary

The focus of the content in previous chapters is aimed at direct service practitioners. Direct service practitioners "know where the client is" and how client/consumer needs can be met in a meaningful way. They also know better about client patterns of behavior, their ups and downs, successes and failures and are more familiar with the day-to-day activities of clients/consumers as opposed to middle management personnel and agency directors. The flip side of this scenario, however, is that many times the direct social work practitioner sees client/consumer needs from a rather narrow perspective. It may be difficult to participate in agency policy change when the organization is a large bureaucracy, wherein function, communication, and authority is well-defined and executed and staff are pigeon-holed in one service unit. Perhaps the geographic setting—urban rather than rural—makes communication among the professional staff more difficult as urban agencies employ many workers as opposed to rural ones that hire two or three professionals who perform both administrative and direct service responsibilities. Perhaps workers are members of a union or an employee association and are constrained to bring about change on an individual basis.

It is important for the direct social work practitioner to educate him or herself about the larger organization and to form alliances with everyone possible within that organization. It takes effort, commitment, time, and energy to secure these alliances, but it may be worth it. Direct service staff can learn by studying the history of the agency, learning about the members of the Board of Directors and the structure of the organization and the kind of people who work there. Never be content to work within your own area. Reach out to form coalitions. Network, listen to the informal communication in the break room, and make yourself available to work on special assignments and task forces. The purpose of these activities is to secure information and feedback from various members of the agency staff and to gain enlightenment about the agency as a whole. The idea, drawn from social systems theory, that the whole is always larger than the sum of its respective parts, is beneficial to keep in mind when analyzing the agency and the people who toil within. When direct social workers participate in many aspects of agency life and get to know other staff, they cannot be accused of harboring a narrow focus by the administration or middle management, especially when they may wish to initiate an agency policy change that requires the support of decision makers in supervisory and administrative positions.

Privatization and managed care procedures define many human service environments at the present time regardless of the type of agency. Administrators and managers are restructuring their agencies to take advantage of contracting with government organizations and maneuvering along with their Boards of Directors and advisory committees to arrange for purchase-of-service agreements from public entities and secure grants from philanthropic foundations. There is increased competition by human service organizations for the same governmental funding in every community across America. Administrators who are concerned about the future of their organizations are looking for creative approaches in service delivery and cost-benefit effectiveness. In managed social services, for example, the provision of bonuses or incentives to "not-for-profits for controlling costs will be a new development, although there has been precedence for this approach in the foster care-adoption field, where the federal government has used bonuses to encourage the states and local communities" (Gibelman & Demone, Jr., 1998). Such incentives may spur workers to create agency policy change. Administrators and middle-management staff can be assisted in their efforts by direct service practitioners who think and feel that they are valued members of the agency team. Direct service social work practitioners are able to contribute information about the needs and outcomes of agency clients/consumers so that administrators and middle-management personnel are motivated to meet the challenges associated with privatization in a committed and accountable manner. An agency environment wherein partnerships between administration and service practitioners are encouraged lends itself to the creation of agency policy change. Needless to say, when direct service workers think that their ideas are valued by administrators, and administrators are respected for their contributions by direct service workers, burnout and apathy may decrease and barriers to change may be reduced. Creativity at all levels of the agency structure will abound!

Important Terms and Phrases

Federalism
Managed care
Mixing and phasing of change strategies
Office model practice

Policy advocacy
Policy practice
Privatization
Purchase of service

Learning Exercises

1. Think of any agency policy that you would like to see changed that would require involvement at the state government level. Then prepare testimony, in writing, that you would give at a public hearing on the issue involved in which you recommend the policy change.

2. For the policy change identified in Exercise 1, list all the agencies and organizations that you feel should be involved in a coalition to influence state government. Try to identify why each of them would be important.

3. Write a sample letter to state legislators to be used by coalition members in their efforts to advocate for the policy change. In that letter, suggest legislative action that would represent a piece of the solution rather than a response to a piece of the problem.

Study Questions

1. Can the Action–Strategy Model of Agency Policy Change be utilized to bring about change at the regional, state, or federal levels?

2. How was Component I of the Action–Strategy Model applied in the case example?

3. How was Component II of the Action–Strategy Model applied in the case example?

4. How was Component III of the Action–Strategy Model applied in the case example?

5. What change strategies were used in the case example?

6. How are social workers attempting to initiate policy change affected by the role of government?

7. In what ways are social workers required to be involved in the political process?

References

Adler, Mortimer J. (1987). *We hold these truths: Understanding the ideas and ideals of the Constitution*. New York: Collier Books.

Appelbaum, Richard P. (1970). *Theories of social change*. Chicago: Markham.

Barker, Robert L. (1991). *The social work dictionary* (2nd ed.). Silver Spring, MD: NASW Press.

—————. (1995). *The social work dictionary* (3rd ed.). Washington, DC: NASW Press.

—————. (1999). *The social work dictionary* (4th ed.). Washington, DC: NASW Press.

Bloom, Martin, Fischer, Joel, & Orme, John G. (1999). *Evaluating practice: Guidelines for the accountable professional*. Boston: Allyn and Bacon.

Boyce, Jim et al. (1997). *Special edition using Microsoft Office 97: Professional bestseller edition*. Indianapolis, IN: Que.

Brager, George, & Holloway, Stephen. (1978). *Changing human service organizations: Politics and practice*. New York: Free Press.

Braybrooke, David, & Lindblom, Charles E. (1963). *A strategy of decision: Policy evaluation as a social process*. New York: Free Press of Glencoe.

Brody, Ralph, & Nair, Murali D. (1998). *Macro practice: A generalist approach* (4th ed.). Wheaton, IL: Gregory Publishing Company.

Burden, Tom. (1998). *Social policy and welfare: A clear guide*. London: Pluto Press.

Calabrese, Andrew, & Burgelman, Jean-Claude (Eds.). (1999). *Communication, citizenship, and social policy: Rethinking the limits of the welfare state*. Lanham, MD: Rowman & Littlefield Publishers.

Chambers, Donald E. (2000). *Social policy and social programs: A method for the practical public policy analyst* (3rd ed.). Boston: Allyn and Bacon.

Council on Social Work Education. (1992). *Curriculum policy statement of 1993*. Washington, DC: Author.

Cox, Archibald. (1987). *The court and the Constitution*. Boston: Houghton Mifflin Company.

Cox, Fred M., Erlich, John L., Rothman, Jack, & Tropman, John E. (Eds.). (1970). *Strategies of community organization; a book of readings*. Itasca, IL: F. E. Peacock Publishers.

—————. (1979). *Strategies of community organization; a book of readings* (3rd ed.). Itasca, IL: F. E. Peacock Publishers.

—————. (Eds.). (1984). *Tactics and techniques of community practice*. Itasca, IL: F. E. Peacock Publishers.

—————. (Eds.). (1987). *Strategies of community organization: Macro practice* (4th ed.). Itasca, IL: F. E. Peacock Publishers.

DeJong, Peter, & Miller, Scott D. (1995). How to interview for client strengths. *Social Work, 40*, 729–736.

Deming, W. Edwards. (1986). *Out of the crisis*. Cambridge, MA: Massachusetts Institute of Technology, Center for Advanced Engineering Study.

Dessler, Gary. (1980). *Organization theory: Integrating structure and behavior*. Englewood Cliffs, NJ: Prentice-Hall.

————. (1986). *Organization theory: Integrating structure and behavior* (2nd ed.). Englewood Cliffs, NJ: Prentice-Hall.

Devore, Wynetta, & Schlesinger, Elfriede G. (1999). *Ethnic-sensitive social work practice* (5th ed.). Boston: Allyn and Bacon.

Diliberto, Gioia. (1999). *A useful woman: The early life of Jane Addams.* New York: Simon & Schuster Trade.

DiNitto, Diana M. (2000). *Social welfare: Politics and public policy* (5th ed.). Boston: Allyn and Bacon.

Dluhy, Milan J. (1981). *Changing the system: Political advocacy for disadvantaged groups.* Beverly Hills, CA: Sage Publications.

Dolgoff, Ralph, Feldstein, Donald, & Skolnik, Louise. (1997). *Understanding social welfare* (4th ed.). New York: Longman.

Drucker, Peter F. (1974). *Management: Tasks, responsibilities, practices.* New York: Harper and Row, Publishers.

DuBois, Brenda, & Miley, Karla Krogsrud. (1992). *Social work: An empowering profession.* Boston: Allyn and Bacon.

Erlich, John L., Rothman, Jack, & Teresa, Joseph G. (1999). *Taking action in organizations and communities* (2nd ed.). Dubuque, IA: Eddie Bowers Publishing, Inc.

Etzioni, Amitai. (1964). *Modern organizations.* Englewood Cliffs, NJ: Prentice-Hall.

Fey, Don. (1995, December). Prelude to a proposal: The value of position papers. *Fund Raising Management, 26,* 45–48.

Fisher, Robert, & Karger, Howard Jacob. (1997). *Social work and community in a private world: Getting out in public.* White Plains, NY: Longman.

Flynn, John P. (1985). *Social agency policy: Analysis and presentation for community practice.* Chicago: Nelson-Hall Publishers.

Friedman, Lawrence M. (1991). *A history of American law.* Birmingham, AL: Gryphon Editions.

Gibbs, Leonard E. (1991). *Scientific reasoning for social workers: Bridging the gap between research and practice.* New York: Macmillan Publishing.

Gibbs, Leonard E., & Gambrill, Eileen. (1998). *Critical thinking for social workers: Exercises for the helping professions.* Thousand Oaks, CA: Pine Forge Press.

Gibelman, Margaret. (1995). *What social workers do.* Washington, DC: NASW Press.

Gibelman, Margaret, & Demone, Jr., Harold (Eds.). (1998). *The privatization of human services.* New York: Springer.

Gibelman, Margaret, & Schervish, Philip H. (1993). *Who we are: The social work labor force as reflected in the NASW membership.* Washington, DC: NASW Press.

Gil, David G. (1998). *Confronting injustice and oppression: Concepts and strategies for social workers.* New York: Columbia University Press.

Glisson, Charles. (2000). Organizational climate and culture. In Rino J. Patti (Ed.), *The handbook of social welfare management.* Thousand Oaks, CA: Sage Publications, Inc.

Gortner, Harold F., Mahler, Julianne, & Nicholson, Jeanne Bell. (1997). *Organization theory: A public perspective* (2nd ed.). Fort Worth, TX: Harcourt Brace College Publishers.

Grant, Gary B., & Grobman, Linda May. (1998). *The social worker's Internet handbook.* Harrisburg, PA: White Hat Communications.

Griffin, Ricky W., & Moorhead, Gregory. (1986). *Organizational behavior.* Boston: Houghton Mifflin Company.

Gummer, Burton. (1998). Current perspectives on diversity in workforce: How diverse is diverse? *Administration in Social Work, 22*(1).

Hall, Richard H. (1991). *Organizations: Structures, processes and outcomes* (5th ed.). Englewood Cliffs, NJ: Prentice Hall.

Hanson, James G., & McCullagh, James G. (1995, Winter). Career choice factors for BSW students: A 10-year perspective. *Journal of Social Work Education, 31,* 28–37.

Hasenfeld, Yeheskel (Ed.). (1992). *Human services as complex organizations.* Newbury Park, CA: Sage Publications.

————. (2000). Social welfare administration and organizational theory. In Rino J. Patti (Ed.), *The handbook of social welfare management*. Thousand Oaks, CA: Sage Publications, Inc.

Haynes, Karen S., & Mickelson, James S. (2000). *Affecting change: Social workers in the political arena* (4th ed.). Boston: Allyn and Bacon.

Homan, Mark S. (1998). *Rules of the game: Lessons from the field of community change*. Pacific Grove, CA: Brooks/Cole Publishing Company.

————. (1999). *Promoting community change: Making it happen in the real world* (2nd ed.). Pacific Grove, CA: Brooks/Cole Publishing Company.

Horejsi, Charles R., & Garthwait, Cynthia L. (1999). *The social work practicum: A guide and workbook for students*. Boston: Allyn and Bacon.

Huber, George P., & Glick, William H. (Eds.) (1993). *Organizational change and redesign: Ideas and insights for improving performance*. New York: Oxford University Press.

Hu-DeHart, Evelyn. (1999, June). NASW annual leadership meeting, April 1999. *NASW News, 44*(6).

Hudson, Christopher. (2000, Spring/Summer). At the edge of chaos: A new paradigm for social work? *Journal of Social Work Education, 36*(2).

Iglehart, Alfreda P., & Becerra, Rosina M. (1995). *Social services and the ethnic community*. Boston: Allyn and Bacon.

Jansson, Bruce S. (1999). *Becoming an effective policy advocate: From policy practice to social justice* (3rd ed.). Pacific Grove: Brooks/Cole.

Johnson, Louise C. (1992). *Social work practice: A generalist approach* (4th ed.). Boston: Allyn and Bacon.

Johnson, Louise C., Schwartz, Charles L., & Tate, Donald S. (1997). *Social welfare: A response to human need* (4th ed.). Boston: Allyn and Bacon.

Kabagarama, Daisy. (1993). *Breaking the ice: A guide to understanding people from other cultures*. Boston: Allyn and Bacon.

Kahn, Alfred J. (1973). *Social policy and social services*. New York: Random House.

Kahn, Si. (1970). *How people get power: Organizing oppressed communities for action*. New York: McGraw-Hill.

Kardas, Edward P., & Milford, Tommy M. (1996). *Using the Internet for social science research and practice*. Belmont: Wadsworth.

Karger, Howard Jacob, & Levine, Joanne. (1999). *The Internet and technology for the human services*. New York: Longman.

Karger, Howard Jacob, & Stoesz, David. (1994). *American social welfare policy: A pluralist approach* (2nd ed.). New York: Longman.

————. (1998). *The Internet and social welfare policy*. Accompanied by *American social welfare policy: A pluralist approach* (3rd ed.). New York: Longman.

————. (2002). *American social welfare policy: A pluralist approach* (4th ed.). Boston: Allyn and Bacon.

Karls, James M., & Wandrei, Karin E. (1994). *PIE manual: Person-in-environment system: The PIE classification system for social functioning problems*. Washington, DC: NASW Press.

Katz, Daniel, & Kahn, Robert L. (1966). *The social psychology of organizations*. New York: John Wiley & Sons.

Kazin, Michael. (1999, September 26). "Addams family values." *New York Times*, sec. 7, p. 24, col. 2.

Kettner, Peter M., Daley, John M., & Nichols, Ann Weaver. (1985). *Initiating change in organizations and communities: A macro practice model*. Monterey, CA: Brooks/Cole Publishing.

Kiritz, Norton. (1988). *Program planning and proposal writing: Introductory version*. Los Angeles: The Grantsmanship Center.

Kretzman, John P., & McKnight, J. L. (1993). *Building communities from the inside out: A path toward finding and mobilizing a community's assets*. Evanston, IL: Northwestern University, Center for Urban Affairs and Policy Research.

Landon, Pamela S. with Feit, Marvin. (1999). *Generalist social work practice*. Dubuque, IA: Eddie Bowers Publishing.

Lathrop, Donald. (n.d.). *The preparation and use of position statement in social work practice*.

Lewin, Kurt. (1951). *Field theory in social science*. New York: Harper & Brothers Publishers.

Linzer, Norman. (1999). *Resolving ethical dilemmas in social work practice*. Boston: Allyn and Bacon.

Macht, Mary Wirtz, & Ashford, José B. (1991). *Introduction to social work and social welfare*. New York: Macmillan Publishing.

Mandiberg, James M. (Ed.). (2000). *Stand! Introduction to social work*. Bellevue, IA: Coursewise Publishing, Inc.

Martin, Lawrence. (2000). The environmental context of social welfare administration. In Rino J. Patti (Ed.), *The handbook of social welfare management*. Thousand Oaks, CA: Sage Publications, Inc.

Martin, Lawrence L., & Kettner, Peter M. (1996). *Measuring the performance of human service programs*. Thousand Oaks, CA: Sage Publications.

McInnis-Dittrich, Kathleen. (1994). *Integrating social welfare policy & social work practice*. Pacific Grove, CA: Brooks/Cole Publishing Company.

McKenzie, Jr., John, & Goldman, Robert. (1999). *The student edition of MINITAB for Windows manual: Release 12*. Reading, MA: Addison-Wesley.

McKinnon, K., Cournos, F., & Stanley, B. (1989). Rivers in practice: Clinicians' assessments of patient's decision-making capacity. *Hospital and Community Psychiatry, 40*(11), 1159–1162.

Meenaghan, Thomas M., Washington, Robert O., & Ryan, Robert M. (1982). *Macro practice in the human services: An introduction to planning, administration, evaluation, and community organizing components of practice*. New York: Free Press.

Midgley, James. (1999, March). Growth, redistribution, and welfare: Toward social investment. *Social Services Review*, 3–21.

Miley, Karla Krogsrud, O'Melia, Michael, & DuBois, Brenda. (1998). *Generalist social work practice: An empowering approach* (2nd ed.). Boston: Allyn and Bacon.

Moroney, R. M. (1977). Needs assessment for human services. In Wayne F. Anderson, Bernard J. Frieden, & Michael J. Murphy (Eds.), *Managing human services*. Washington, DC: International City Managers Association.

National Association of Social Workers. (1973). *Standards for social service manpower*. Washington, DC: NASW Press.

————. (1981). *NASW standards for the classification of social work practice*. Silver Springs, MD: NASW Press.

————. (1996). *NASW code of ethics*. Silver Springs, MD: NASW Press.

————. (1999). *NASW code of ethics*. Silver Springs, MD: NASW Press.

————. (2000). Membership Services. Personal communication. Silver Springs, MD.

————. (2001, June). Standards for Cultural Competence in Social Work Practice. Prepared by the NASW National Committee on Racial and Ethnic Diversity. Approved by the Board of Directors, June 23, 2001.

Netting, F. Ellen, Kettner, Peter M., & McMurtry, Steven L. (1993). *Social work macro practice*. New York: Longman.

————. (1998). *Social work macro practice* (2nd ed.). New York: Longman.

Neugeboren, Bernard. (1991). *Organization, policy, and practice in the human services*. New York: Haworth Press.

Ouchi, William G. (1981). *Theory Z: How American business can meet the Japanese challenge*. Reading, MA: Addison-Wesley.

————. (1993). *Theory Z: How American business can meet the Japanese challenge* (2nd ed.). New York: Avon.

Patterson, David A. (2000). *Personal computer applications in the social services*. Boston: Allyn and Bacon.

Patti, Rino J. (1974). Organizational resistance and change: The view from below. In *Making organizations work for people*. Washington, DC: National Association of Social Workers, Inc.

Pawlak, Edward. (1979). Organizational maneuvering: Intra-organizational change tactics. In *Strategies of community organization; a book of readings* (3rd ed.). Itasca, IL: F. E. Peacock Publishers.

Perkins, Kathleen, & Tice, Carolyn. (2000). A strengths perspective in practice: Older people and mental health challenges. In James M. Mandiberg (Eds.), *Stand! Introduction to social work*. Bellevue, IA: Coursewise Publishing Inc.

Peters, Thomas J., & Waterman, Jr., Robert H. (1982). *In search of excellence: Lessons from America's best-run companies*. New York: Harper & Row.

Piven, Frances Fox, & Cloward, Richard A. (1971). *Regulating the poor; the function of public welfare*. New York: Pantheon Books.

Popple, Philip R., & Leighninger, Leslie. (1996). *Social work, social welfare, and American society* (3rd ed.). Boston: Allyn and Bacon.

————. (1998). *The policy-based profession: An introduction to social welfare policy for social workers*. Boston: Allyn and Bacon.

Prasad, Anshmen, & Prasad, Pushkala. (1998). Everyday struggles at the workplace: The nature and implications of routine resistance in contemporary organizations. *Research in the Sociology of Organizations, 15*, 225–227.

Rae, Ann, & Mellendorf, Scott. (1998). Linking social work practice and social welfare policy in communities and organizations with scientific reasoning and the world wide web. A paper presented at the Joint World Congress of International Federation of Social Workers and the International Association of Schools of Social Work, Jerusalem, Israel.

Reamer, Frederic G. (1998). *Social work research and evaluation skills: A case-based, user-friendly approach*. New York: Columbia University Press.

————. (1998). The evolution of social work ethics. *Social Work, 43*, 488–500.

Reid, William J. (1964, December). Interagency co-ordination in delinquency prevention and control. *Social Service Review, 38*, 418–422.

Resnick, Herman, & Patti, Rino J. (Eds.). (1980). *Change from within: Humanizing social welfare organizations*. Philadelphia: Temple University Press.

Ripple, Lilian, with Alexander, Ernestina, & Polemis, Bernice W. (1964). *Motivation, capacity, and opportunity: Studies in casework theory and practice*. Chicago: School of Social Service Administration, University of Chicago.

Rossi, Peter H., Freeman, Howard E., & Lipsey, Mark W. (1999). *Evaluation: A systematic approach*. Thousand Oaks, CA: Sage Publications.

Rothman, Jack. (1979). Three models of community organization practice, their mixing and phasing. In Fred M. Cox, John L. Erlich, Jack Rothman & John E. Tropman (Eds.), *Strategies of community organization; a book of readings* (3rd ed.). Itasca, IL: F. E. Peacock Publishers.

Rubin, Allen, & Babbie, Earl. (1993). *Research methods for social work*. Pacific Grove, CA: Brooks/Cole.

Ryan, William. (1976). *Blaming the victim*. New York: Vintage Books.

Saleebey, Dennis (Ed.). (1997). *The strengths perspective in social work practice* (2nd ed.). New York: Longman.

Schwartz, Bernard. (1977). *The great rights of mankind: A history of the American Bill of Rights*. New York: Oxford University Press.

Sherraden, Michael W. (1991). *Assets and the poor: A new American welfare policy*. Armonk, NY: M. E. Sharpe.

Simon, Barbara Levy. (1994). *The empowerment tradition in American social work: A history*. New York: Columbia University Press.

Social work speaks. (2000). Silver Spring, MD: National Association of Social Workers.

Solomon, Barbara Bryant. (1976). *Black empowerment: Social work in oppressed communities*. New York: Columbia University Press.

Thaves, Bob. (1999, October 7). Frank and Ernest. *The Saginaw News*, p. 8C.

Titmuss, Richard. (1963). *Essays on the welfare system*. Boston: Beacon Press.

Tropman, John E. (1995). Value conflicts and decision making: Analysis and Resolution. In John E. Tropman, John L. Erlich, & Jack Rothman (Eds.), *Tactics and techniques of community intervention* (3rd ed.). Itasca, IL: F.E. Peacock Publishers.

—————. (1999). *Personal communication*. Ann Arbor, MI: The University of Michigan, School of Social Work.

United States Constitution. Preamble, Article I, Section VIII.

Vernon, Robert, & Lynch, Darlene. (2000). *Social work and the web*. East Dubuque, IL: Wadsworth Thomson Learning.

Vonk, M. Elizabeth. (2001, July). Cultural competence for transracial adoptive parents. *Social Work, 46*, 246–255.

Warheit, George J., Bell, Robert A., & Schwab, John J. (1977). *Planning for change: Needs assessment approaches*. Washington, DC: National Institute of Mental Health.

Warren, Keith, Franklin, Cynthia, & Streeter, Calvin L. (1998). New directions in systems theory: Chaos and complexity. *Social Work, 43*, 357–372.

Warren, Roland L. (1972). *The community in America* (2nd ed.). Chicago: Rand McNally.

—————. (1973). *Truth, love and social change, and other essays on community change*. Chicago: Rand McNally.

—————. (1977). *Social change and human purpose: Toward understanding and action*. Chicago: Rand McNally.

Weick, Karl E., & Quinn, Robert E. (1999). Organizational change and development. *Annual Review of Psychology, 50*, 361–386.

Weil, Marie. (1996). *Community practice: Conceptual models*. New York and London: The Haworth Press.

—————. (1996, September). Community building: Building community practice. *Social Work, 41*, 481–499.

Weil, Marie, & Gamble, Dorothy N. (1995). Community practice models. In *The encyclopedia of social work* (19th ed.). Washington, DC: NASW.

Weinbach, Robert W. (1998). *The social worker as manager: A practical guide to success* (3rd ed.). Boston: Allyn and Bacon.

Weinbach, Robert W., & Grinnell, Jr., Richard M. (1998). *Statistics for social workers*. New York: Longman.

Whitaker, William H., & Federico, Ronald C. (1997). *Social welfare in today's world* (2nd ed.). New York: McGraw-Hill.

Williams, J. Clifton, & Huber, George P. (1986). *Human behavior in organizations* (3rd ed.). Cincinnati: South-Western Publishing Co.

Wolk, James L., Pray, Jackie E., Weismiller, Toby, & Dempsey, David. (1996, Winter). Political practice: Educating social work students for policymaking. *Journal of Social Work Education, 32*(1), 91–100.

Wyers, Norman. (1991). Policy-practice in social work: Models and issues. *Journal of Social Work Education, 27*(3), 241–250.

Zastrow, Charles. (1989). *Social work with groups: Using the class as a group leadership laboratory*. Chicago: Nelson-Hall Publishers.

Index